Attitude Shifting™

"Choosing To Change Your Attitude
Will Change Your Life!"

Gibbs Williams Ph.D.
Herbert Williams

© 2012 by Herbert R. Williams & Gibbs A. **Williams Ph.D.**

All rights reserved.

All Rights Reserved.   No part of this publication may be reproduced in any form or by any means, including scanning, photocopying, or otherwise without prior written permission of the copyright holder.

Disclaimer and Terms of Use: The author and publisher of Self Help Product Reviews disclaim any warranties (express or implied), merchantability, or fitness of materials expressed for any particular purpose. The author and publisher shall in no event be held liable to any party for any direct, indirect, punitive, special, incidental or other consequential damages arising directly or indirectly from any use of this material, which is provided as is, and without warranties.

First Printing, 2012

ISBN 9781468129977

Printed in the United States of America

Table of Contents

TABLE OF CONTENTS ... 3
WE ARE ALL OUR ... 6
BROTHERS' KEEPERS ... 6
GENESIS OF A THEORY ... 6
OUR PHILOSOPHY, RE... ATTAINING AND SUSTAINING THE GOOD LIFE ... 9
   THE PRESSING ISSUE OF OUR TIME ... 9
   WHAT THIS BOOK IS REALLY ABOUT ... 14
WHO IS THIS BOOK REALLY FOR? ... 18
WHY ATTITUDE SHIFTING™ IS UNIQUE? ... 19
WHAT YOU WILL DISCOVER ... 22
ARE DRUGS REALLY THE ANSWER? ... 24
   RESEARCH FINDINGS ... 25
   PHARMACEUTICALS ARE A HUGE BUSINESS ... 26
   A MOST REVEALING VIDEO ... 28
   IMPLICATIONS OF THE PLACEBO EFFECT STUDIES ... 28
   MORE IMPORTANT IMPLICATIONS OF THE PLACEBO STUDIES ... 30
THE LOSS OF SOCIAL SUPPORT SYSTEMS IN MANAGING STRESS AND ANXIETY ... 31
   THE WORLD HEALTH REPORT ... 32
   IMPLICATIONS FOR ATTITUDE SHIFTING™ ... 34
OUR RADICAL CONCLUSION ... 36
   WHAT GUIDES US ... 37
ASSESSING WHAT'S WRONG ... 40
   WHAT IS STRESS? ... 40
HOW STRESS FEELS ... 41
   SOME SYMPTOMS ASSOCIATED WITH STRESS ... 44
   LOW AND HIGH LEVELS OF STRESS ... 45
WHAT IS ANXIETY? ... 47
   WHAT CAUSES ANXIETY ... 47
DEPRESSION ... 54
   WHAT IS DEPRESSION? ... 54
   SYMPTOMS ASSOCIATED WITH DEPRESSION ... 55
   THE CAUSES OF DEPRESSION ... 55
   HOW THEY AFFECT US ... 56
   PRACTICAL AND PSYCHOLOGICAL TRIGGERS ... 57
   INTERNAL STRESSORS ... 58
   EXAMPLES OF INTERNAL STRESSORS INCLUDE: ... 58
      Fears ... *58*
UNCERTAINTY ... 58
   Pessimism ... *58*

Unrealistic Expectations *58*
Blurred ego boundaries *59*
Contents of Consciousness Boundaries *59*

CHOICE AND CHANGE-THERE IS A DIFFERENCE 61
    THE DIFFERENCE BETWEEN CHOICE AND CHANGE 61

JOE'S STORY 63

ARE YOU YOUR BROTHER'S KEEPER? 69

THE NEED FOR A HELPER 69

THE HELPER DEFINED 70
    WHO IS A HELPER? 71

THE ROLE OF THE HELPER 71

ATTITUDES OF THE EFFECTIVE HELPER 72

STEPS IN BECOMING AN EFFECTIVE HELPER 73

WHEN THEY NEED MORE THAN JUST A FRIEND 74

ENGAGING A PERSON IN NEED OF HELP 76

THE DISCOVERY PROCESS 78

IMPLEMENTING THE DISCOVERY PROCESS 79

OBSERVING THEIR APPARENT STATES OF STRESS 79
    THE CASE OF JOHN 79
    INITIAL DISCOVERY QUESTIONS 80
    FURTHER DISCOVERY QUESTIONS 81

STEP 1 - DISCOVERING THE SURFACE ISSUE IN EVERY CRISIS 83
    MONEY, MONEY, MONEY 84
    JUST PLAIN PRESSURED 84
    MY JOB IS A PAIN IN THE A 85
    I'M NOT GOING TO TAKE IT ANYMORE 85
    TIME ISN'T WHAT IT USED TO BE 86
    THE IMPORTANCE OF STAYING HEALTHY 87
    WHO AM I REALLY? 87
        Major Life Changes *88*
        Environmental Issues *89*
        Unpredictable Events Issues *89*
        Social Issues *89*
    WAR IS HELL 89
        If I Could Only Stop! *90*
    MY WEIGHT IS KILLING ME 90
        Death and Dying Issues *90*
        Marital *90*
    SEXUAL ISSUES 91
        Children *91*

STEP 2: SHIFTING YOUR FOCUS 95

STEP 3: IDENTIFYING THE ATTITUDE OF THE STRESSED 98

STEP 4 – THE NEED TO SHIFT FROM A NEGATIVE ATTITUDE TO POSITIVE *99*

IT WORKS LIKE MAGIC!	102
HOW ATTITUDES ARE SHIFTED FROM NEGATIVE TO POSITIVE.	102
TAKE A BATH or EXTENDED SHOWER	110
SPECIFIC ATTITUDE SHIFTERS	113
ABOUT THE USE OF EXERCISES	113
A PRE THREE STEP PROCESS	115
APPLYING SPECIFIC ATTITUDE SHIFTERS™	115
EXERCISE -M1- IDENTIFYING YOUR ATTITUDES TO ANXIETY, DEPRESSION, FRUSTRATION, AND STRESS	117
EXERCISE – M2 – LEARNING TO BEAR INCREASING DOSAGES OF FRUSTRATION	119
EXERCISE – M3 - EXPERIENCE MAKING CHOICES	122
EXERCISE – M4 – ON YOUR MARK, GET SET, GO!	124
EXERCISE – M5 - LEARNING HOW TO BE PATIENT - (DELAYING ACTION)	127
THE UNMOTIVATED	129
CAUSES OF A LACK OF MOTIVATION	130
FEW PEOPLE WILL RESIST, AT LEAST GIVING THE EXERCISES A TRY!	132
EXERCISES FOR THE UN-MOTIVATED	133
EXERCISE -UM1- CREATING HOPE IN A LIFE FILLED WITH NEGATIVITY.	134
EXERCISE – UM 2 - LEARNING ABOUT REGULATING & DE-REGULATING YOUR SELF ESTEEM	136
THE PROCESS OF SELF ESTEEM REGULATION (POSITIVE AND NEGATIVE)	137
EXERCISE –UM3 – HOW DOES REALITY REALLY LOOK?	146
CONVENTIONAL APPROACHES TO STRESS MANAGEMENT	147
APPROACHES DEFINED	147
THE LIST	148
SOME LIMITATIONS-RE CONVENTIONAL EXERCISES	153
ADDITIONAL RESOURCES	159

As you read this guide you will notice our little detective. He represents information that might dig a little deeper, just might be a little more technical or might expand the thought a little more than the average, none professional, is looking for. It won't be necessary for you to read this information. Just learn the techniques and how to put into practice the concepts of **Attitude Shifting**™.

We Are All Our Brothers' Keepers

Genesis of a Theory

I am very excited. It has been exactly two years that my brother and I conceived of an idea to create a Resource Guide to aid mental health workers and any potential Helpers to aid those in need to effectively cope with their stress, anxiety, frustration, and depression without the use of medication.

The context is important. I love my brother but he has been a hard-headed realist who under "normal" conditions would never ever consider going to a psychotherapist. Like many hard nosed realists he is a believer in only using your will power to "get over it."

Thus it was shocking when he called on Thanksgiving telling me he was out of the hospital having received a multiple bypass two days before, alive, but scared to death, obviously stressed out. He thought I would understand.

He indicated that while the operation was supposed to be a complete success he was getting the same feelings he had just before his heart issues. I instantly thought he might be having a panic attack [often confused with symptoms of a heart attack] and asked him if I could do my "shrink" thing. He said that was the reason why he was calling me.

In talking together for the next few hours it was clear he was soaking up the concepts I gave him including how anxiety and stress feel, what causes them, his attitude toward his associated fantasies, how they affect his self esteem regulation and the likes....

Much of what I told him instantly resonated – but other material perplexed him because of the technical language I used. As we talked he got increasingly more excited applying the concepts I gave him as psychological tools.

In the next day's conversation, clearly impressed, he said he finally understood what I do for a living. Generalizing from his experience he rightly figured there must be countless people, who overwhelmed with negative feelings like him, would be grateful to be able to discuss his troubles with 'a caring brother [not necessarily a trained professional].

He also suggested we write a resource Guide. We did exactly that collaborating for the last two years on a daily basis.

During these last two years my brother and myself have thought carefully about identifying exactly what it was that resulted in our initial two hour talk being so transformative for both of us.

I was able to distill forty-four years of personal and professional experience. He was able to transform my sometimes too abstract language into clear enough words such that a concerned layman could effectively use the material to be potentially helpful.

We have concluded that what was most helpful in our first talk was more than talking together – it was 'special talk' communicated in a 'special way' that is the reason why we believe anyone who wishes to being maximally helpful to those in crisis would likely benefit by reading and applying this resource manual.

~ Gibbs A Williams Ph.D.

OUR PHILOSOPHY, RE... ATTAINING and SUSTAINING the GOOD LIFE

Experience teaches us that life, from one perspective, appears to be a never ending series of obstacles to be mastered. This fact strongly implies that one key to living the good life is for each of us to become expert problem solvers.

The Attitude Shifting™ resource guide offers highly effective tools for creating the necessary psychological infrastructure (a solid identity and strong ego) as the absolute prerequisite for implementing effective problem solving both short term and for more than you would think, long term relief.

The Pressing Issue of Our Time

A pressing issue for people in a state of crisis, whether it is stress, depression, anxiety or any variation thereof, is that they want, need, and absolutely require immediate attention.

This generally does not happen.

It typically takes weeks before people in crisis can be seen by professional care givers. This guide provides effective methods for first responders to greatly reduce this time gap.

For example, a newly registered Veteran once diagnosed at the VA is typically told to return to his first counseling appointment a month later. This four week time delay before services are provided can be catastrophic.

We hope to help fill this critical space by enabling first responders to immediately intervene thus exponentially increasing the probable odds for successful crises intervention.

This guide is written for all lay and professionals who wish to help people in need of help to effectively cope with anxiety, depression, frustration and stress without the use of drugs.

Regardless of whether you're reading this book because you have an issue or you are in a position to help others with their issues, the use of **Attitude Shifting**™ will be empowering for everyone.

We've concluded that most of the self-help books and tapes are missing a crucial step…a step that you and they must take in order to achieve the relief and controlled order you and they desperately seek.

They'll read the latest book, listen to the most popular TV Guru, often pop the most recently advertised pill endorsed by the pharmaceutical companies who make them (frequently with positive benefits).

They will try various methods offering 'exercises' designed to reduce the painful symptoms of stress, anxiety, depression, and frustration, many of which result in notable relief. But in practically all cases the relief that comes from symptom reduction is short lived. Underneath is a feeling of overwhelming 'stuckness' as the person feels trapped in a state of 'negative inertia.' What's happening?

Our answer is: You are simply looking in the wrong direction for the answer to your concerns. You believe that the surface issue (i.e. losing your job) is your primary problem whereas it is actually a symptom of a deeper problem which is your negative attitudes towards the accompanying overwhelming emotional reactions to your surface issue (i.e. feeling trapped – unable to act due to immobilizing panic anxiety).

To obtain long term mastery over the feelings of anxiety, depression, frustration, and stress you have to assume the responsibility of addressing causes not symptoms by making a CHOICE to change your ATTITUDE. To do so you must read this book.

To significantly change, you simply have to understand the concept, learn the methods and practice the exercises.

We know you are skeptical, but believe us thousands of people have chosen to change their attitude and in so doing, changed their lives, leaving their stress behind.

Read on…the pathway to many more hours and days of relief are just a few words away!

What This Book Is Really About

Human beings wish to maximize pleasure and minimize pain. Developmental psychology teaches that all newborns start their lives desiring to get both what they want and when they want it without experiencing any delay (frustration). This ideal state of perfection (perfect ease/pure pleasure) is experienced as bliss. The desire to live a life of pure pleasure (dominating childhood awareness) is referred to as the pleasure principle.

Adults, like children, also want to live a life of pure pleasure. However, - internal and external limitations being an inevitable fact of every person's life – forces adults to make necessary compromises between striving to fulfill the impossible fantasy of perfection versus accepting inevitable realistic limitations in order to live relatively balanced lives.

The awareness of inevitable life limitations, experienced as painful 'negative feelings' and the need to cope with them, is referred to as the reality principle.)

Included on every person's list of so called 'negative' feelings are: anxiety, depression, frustration, and tension.

Other so-called negative feelings are: not knowing, ambiguity, ambivalence, complexity, fear, shame and guilt.

A necessary requirement for a person to be able to maintain a relative sense of balance when threatened by internal and or external limitations is the presence of a strong sense of personal identity (the psychological structure of the self) and a strong ego (the voice of reason).

If a person lacks adequate psychological structures [i.e. a solid self and a strong ego] they are vulnerable to being overwhelmed by negative affects particularly those of frustration, anxiety, depression, and or tension (stress).

When life limitations are experienced as overwhelming one feels as if they are thrown off balance typically referred to as a state of crisis. A person in crisis describes himself as feeling like a lost child wishing to be rescued - literally taken by the hand by a secure supportive adult.

People in a state of crisis are most in need of someone who will actively come to their aide to help them restore their lost sense of balance. This proactive process of helping people in crisis is referred to as crisis intervention.

By far the primary aim of nearly all of the conventional approaches in coping with crises has been their focus on relieving the pain associated with symptoms.

However, breakthrough findings of relatively recent research, and practical experience, indicates that <u>the most effective crisis intervention is that which addresses underlying causes rather than simply focusing on symptom reduction.</u>

The underlying cause of psychological crisis is essentially a negative attitude to those feelings experienced as overwhelming.

If this basic assumption is accurate it follows that the most effective crisis intervention will be focused on shifting attitudes towards inevitable realistic limitations from negative to positive.

Attitude Shifting™ is dedicated to assisting First Responders to help stressed people get 'Unstuck" by teaching them how to change their attitudes enabling

Attitude Shifting™

them to move in a positive and less stressful direction utilizing empathy, trust, and verbal communication.

Who Is This Book Really For?

- Interested lay people who have tried but failed to find an effective permanent way to cope with their frustration, stress, depression, and anxiety.

- *Professionals directly and indirectly seeing patients who wish to be more effective in helping them learn how to best manage their experiences of stress, anxiety, depression, and frustration.*

- Any caring person (Helper) who would like to be helpful in lending a helping hand to those who appear to be suffering from stress, depression, and anxiety.

- ✓ Appreciating the fact that both patients and therapists are 'stuck' at various points along a continuum of managing stress and anxiety, this Guide enables anyone to immediately go to the place that seems most relevant to addressing their particular need.

Why Attitude Shifting™ Is Unique?

- Appreciating the fact that some responders want as much theory as they are able to obtain, whereas others want just enough material to effectively intervene: this guideline is written for both professional and lay potential first responders.

- We continue on from where most guides leave off.

- Rather than aim only at short-term symptom relief we aim to provide knowledge of underlying causes resulting in a prescription for life long coping.

- Aware that people in crisis often present with an 'avalanche' of problems, we enable the first responder to quickly identify the core problem in each specific 'case.'

- People in crises initially complain about feeling quintessentially stuck (helpless). **ATTITUDE SHIFTING**™ provides a step by step method for both lay and professional first responders (Helpers) to assist the person in crisis to get unstuck.

- Aware that people in crisis want immediate relief from their overwhelming painful feelings (anxiety, frustration, depression, stress and helplessness) we provide guidelines for accomplishing this task.

- We provide guidelines for first responders to identify, approach, connect, establish a working alliance of trust and collaboration, naming specific words to use, and upon what and when to focus.

- We provide a representative list of basic issues (IE. financial issues, marital issues, work related issues etc.) which trigger crisis situations.

- We provide a step by step description of how the first responder best moves the person in crisis from first focusing on his/her outside (external, surface) issue (stressor) to then focusing on the person's inside (internal, deeper) emotional response to the trigger issue.

We provide specific Attitude Shifters™ (exercises), to be utilized as psychological 'tools', enabling the person under stress to actively and effectively manage his/her painful feelings thereby restoring a lost sense of balance and accompanying empowerment.

In focusing on the above tasks, the theory of ATTITUDE SHIFTING™ takes the position that these so called "negative" feelings (anxiety, depression, and stress) should not be thought of as pathological symptoms to be suppressed; but, rather as normal psychological, reactions to stressful life events should be mastered.

There are additional benefits to all concerned in following this pathway towards effective management of stress anxiety, and depression. While it is a fact that the convergence of 'negative feelings' often feels overwhelming, the greater truth is, if tolerated, you (a potential responder) and those in need of help, will have a golden opportunity to connect with your unique creative process.

Your creative process potentially allows you to become an expert in effective problem solving – the key to attaining and sustaining a life filled with meaningful connections – the pathway in obtaining and sustaining peace of mind.

The authors of this guide believe that if people are in tune with the signals sent from their basic instincts they will know exactly what to do and when to do it in aiding them to adequately resolve what initially are experienced as overwhelming unsolvable problems.

What You Will Discover

- ✓ Those principles and facts which are most important in effectively coping with anxiety, depression, frustration, and stress.
- ✓ How to create and maintain an atmosphere most conducive to helping the stressed effectively cope with anxiety, frustration, and stress and a feeling of helplessness.
- ✓ To identify frustration, stress and anxiety both from the inside out and the outside in.
- ✓ To identify triggers that set off anxiety, depression, frustration, and stress.
- ✓ To identify the process that automatically leads either to self-esteem regulation or crisis.
- ✓ To learn how to keep steady under internal and external pressure.

- ✓ How to attain and sustain a positive attitude to normal and inevitable stressful events.
- ✓ When stuck, learn to connect with and utilize both your own and the other person's unique creative process in the service of effective problem resolution.
- ✓ When and to whom to refer the person in need.
- ✓ How to identify the core reasons for their distress.
- ✓ What responsibilities you have in the helping process to increase the probability of your eventual success.

Are Drugs Really The Answer?

Many readers at this point are likely to question: aren't the right drugs the best answer for these problems?

As you will see, scientific research strongly suggests that for many who suffer from overwhelming stress, anxiety, depression and frustration drugs are not necessarily the most effective way to cope.

Indeed for many prescribed drugs, the 'cure' because of severe side effects may be worse than the 'illness.'

One of our basic assumptions is that while medication is indeed necessary for some people we both agree that the "pop a pill" mentality is too pervasive and that what is shamefully underplayed is the highly significant contribution made by a person's attitudes.

This Guide identifies and focuses on causes of stress, and anxiety, and depression for long lasting mastery rather than simply aiming to achieve short-term symptom relief most commonly by the use of drugs.

Research Findings

Research studies indicate that while drugs are the most widely used means of coping with anxiety, depression, and stress they have major limitations in that they only reduce symptoms rather than deal with causality as well as having major harmful side effects.

WARNING!

If you listen carefully at the end of each ad, you will hear a long list of potentially harmful side effects which raises the question - "Is the cure potentially worse than the disease?"

Pharmaceuticals are a Huge Business

One report states that "More than $24 billion dollars worth of antidepressants and antipsychotic drugs were dispensed in 2008-almost a 48-fold increase since 1986 (Pringle, 2006; Elias, 2009).

Such expenditure would employ 240,000 psychotherapists earning an annual income of $100,000 to provide 6 million hours of psychotherapy averaging 25 client-hours a week.

These figures do not include what would be possible using the additional revenue generated by the sales of anti-anxiety, hypnotic, and psycho-stimulant medications.

How has the disease model for emotional disorders become the dominant philosophy causing so many people to use neuro-pharmaceuticals as the best defense against emotional and behavioral symptoms?

The system has organized itself around a single simple assumption: mental disorders are a chronic condition resulting from a diseased brain that requires expert medical treatment in the form of mass-produced pharmaceuticals (Kuppin & Carpiano, 2006).

The pharmaceutical industry relies on academic psychiatrists to produce evidence that supports their medications. Academic psychiatry depends on the pharmaceutical industry for research grants, draws up treatment protocols, and sets the agenda for the psychiatric profession specifically and the mental health profession in general.

Insurance companies rely on pharmaceuticals to contain costs (and limit psychotherapy sessions), and reimbursement depends on a diagnosis of a diseased brain.

All these groups work to provide, in their view, vital services for one another, with the goal being improved mental health for everyone.

As a capitalistic system with a drive toward greater profits, modern healthcare has evolved into a sickness care system.

A Most Revealing Video

http://youtu.be/Zihdr36WVi4

Research studies assessing the therapeutic benefits in reducing stress, anxiety and depression are discovering that a great percentage of the positive effects of the drugs are due less to the drugs themselves than to the placebo effect.

Implications of the Placebo Effect Studies

The essence of the effectiveness of the placebo effect is that it generates hope in a person resulting in a heightened expectation of a favorable outcome.

Since the positive effects of anti depressants is estimated to be 75% due to the placebo effect this lends strong evidence that the right attitude is critically important in the management of depression etc.

Because the placebo effect is based upon expectations and conditioning, the effect disappears if the patient is told that their expectations are unrealistic, or that the placebo intervention is ineffective.

A conditioned pain reduction can be totally removed when its placebos in a trial of anti-depressants, that "Once the trial was over and the patients who had been given placebos were told as much, they quickly deteriorated.
http://en.wikipedia.org/wiki/Placebo

There is no disagreement that body chemistry has a direct causal effect on the mind in the form of feelings, and emotions. This means that for some people because of their unique risk to reward ratio a prescription for drugs is absolutely necessary for them to effectively cope with anxiety, depression and stress even facing the potentiality of their experiencing serious side effects.

However, drug research studies [notably placebo studies] also indicate that because the body and the mind are interactive, causality is a two way street.

While physiology can be seen as causing psychological symptoms, it is equally true that psychological factors (i.e. attitudes) can cause a reduction in physiological symptoms. This means that while body chemistry affects the mind, it is also true that the mind affects body chemistry.

More Important Implications of the Placebo Studies

In this connection, although medication is a seductive choice, it would be far more helpful to a person in need of help if they can be encouraged to learn how to tolerate their aversive negative affects. This of course depends upon a complainer's relative courage and desire to learn.

If they are ready, willing and able to initially tough it out and learn how to manage their feelings by applying their own effort, this, of course, is a considerably better outcome by empowering the person rather than encouraging a life-long dependency on medication. The essence of this point of view is embodied in the following question: Is it as better for a child who wants to learn how to fish be given a fish by his father or taught how to fish?

Research Studies Lending Scientific Legitimacy in Supporting the Theory of Attitude Shifting™

Support for the theory of Attitude Shifting™ is widespread. The following studies are representative of a growing interest in understanding their causes with the aim of finding some long lasting cures which ideally are both free of debilitating side effects and are cost effective as well.

The loss of social support systems in managing stress and anxiety

Statistics indicates that stress, anxiety, and depression have been increasing all over the world reaching epidemic proportions. Stress is increasing to the point of a worldwide epidemic affecting some of the most ordinary jobs.

Waitresses in Sweden, teachers in Japan, postal workers in America, bus drivers in Europe and assembly line workers everywhere are all showing increasing signs of job stress, the organization said Monday. Pressure to keep up with machines, no say about the job and low pay for long hours have left millions of workers burned out, accident-prone.

One would think that they would be expected to have high levels of anxiety, stress and depression given numerous stressors including, continuing wars, vulnerability to contagious diseases such as malaria, poverty, natural disasters (Tsunamis).

These conditions have always existed but the levels of stress, anxiety and depression have remained relatively stable until recently.

Attitude Shifting™ confronts the problem of why stress and anxiety are escalating worldwide and how these two issues can be substantially relieved for a great number of the world's population, *not primarily by the use of pills and medications*, but by taking the time and initiative to understand ourselves and others thereby compensating for lost social support systems.

The World Health Report

The World Health Organization Report on the Increase of Depression in the Third World is due to the wide spread migration that has broken down the social structure.

Previous to the current wave of migration, family and friends have functioned as a support-system for people suffering from these symptoms. [Currently] due to the fact that many migrants, having lost their connection with their familiar support systems, find themselves isolated and alone in coping with stress, anxiety and depression.

This one fact strongly suggests that raising the general level of consciousness would highlight the importance of establishing a needed strong social support system in coping with stress and anxiety.

The essence of <u>effective social support systems</u> is their attitude to engaging those in need of help in coping with anxiety, depression, frustration, and stress.

Implications for Attitude Shifting™

Research and common sense observations indicate there is a pressing need to make up for the increasing world-wide lack of social support systems.

In the United States there is an over reliance on "experts" such as medical doctors, psychiatrists, social workers, psychotherapists et.al. routinely thought to be the people of choice to which people in need of crisis intervention must be 'referred for treatment."

The authors of this manual dispute this myth and are of the strong conviction that much potential benefit can happen pre formal professional referrals.

The authors of this guide are of the strong belief that anxiety, depression, frustration, and stress – contrary to wide spread propaganda put forth by the pharmaceutical companies – are not pathological symptoms which should be suppressed mainly by taking appropriate drugs but are in fact normal psychological feelings accompanying inevitable human limitations. Again, we say; "They are best managed by shifting one's attitude towards them from negative to positive."

Warning!

Please be aware… the reading of this guide does not imply that those who choose to be Helpers applying the principles we outline are automatically qualified to be thought of as professional crisis interventionists.

However we do believe that just as well meaning, caring people have always been helpful in providing necessary social supports –those who read this guide might be expected to do a great deal of effective management of people in need of immediate help in coping with anxiety, frustration, depression, and stress.

Our Radical Conclusion

"Painful feelings of anxiety, depression and frustration are, in fact, good news."

"They are signals the body and brain emit alerting the self that they are experiencing normal limitations that have to be mastered."

"It is the major assumption of this guide - 'Attitude Shifting™ - that effective management of these painful feelings hesitates an attitudinal shift in viewing anxiety, depression, and stress - not as an enemy force to be defended against as bad, - but, embracing these feelings as a potential friend thereby functioning as a starting point in becoming a useful ally."

Powerful organizing principles and concepts will be offered in the service of providing a drug free alternative for professional mental health practitioners, any caring potential responder, and all those in need of a helping hand, towards effectively coping with these natural and inevitable painful experiences.

What Guides Us

- ✓ Some basic facts about stress and anxiety including: what they are, symptoms associated with them, and what causes them.
- ✓ Some myths attributed to stress and anxiety Representative events which trigger stress and anxiety reactions.
- ✓ Some representative anecdotes and situations
- ✓ Questions for both helpers and people needing help
- ✓ What you will learn in reading this course
- ✓ Identifying issues
- ✓ Conventional exercises to reduce stress and anxiety
- ✓ Limitations of conventional exercises
- ✓ Attitude Shifters
- ✓ Choice or Change

There is no magic in effectively managing frustration, depression, stress and anxiety. There must be a readiness, willingness and capability of both the person needing help and a potential helper to engage in a collaborative effort in identifying, exploring and shifting one's initial negative to positive towards that which is initially complained about.

Your creative process potentially allows you to become an expert in effective problem solving – the key to attaining and sustaining a life filled with meaningful connections and obtaining sustained peace of mind.

In shifting attitudes away from anxiety, and stress (also frustration, depression and other painful emotions) the person in need of help gets an immediate shot of hope that he can – with practiced effort – CHANGE his passive helplessness (negative inertia) into active choosing resulting in a feeling of empowerment experienced as positive inertia.

An initial experience of flailing reactivity is converted into an experience of pro active 'I'ness acting - from within. One changes by changing that is choosing to make a change.

Assessing What's Wrong

Whether it is a potential patient consulting their potential new therapist, or a friend in need of help, both will complain about the intrusive effects of anxiety, depression, stress, and, or, frustration.

It is invaluable for the effective responder to be as informed as they can be about the many facets of frustration, depression, stress and anxiety. While most of us know precisely how these emotional states feel there are still many facets which are less commonly known or treated with the respect they deserve.

What Is Stress?

Stress is the feeling of tension (friction) that fills the gap between that which is sought after versus what one actually has. Thus it is the tension between being and desiring. There are countless occasions in daily living that people experience stress.

A few common examples:

- When driving on the highway after a long day at work encountering a 'crazy' driver purposefully cutting you off and all your attempts to get rid of him fail there is often a growing tension experienced as frustrated aggression. If this frustrated aggression persists it can and often does escalate into 'road rage.'

- Another example of stress in the workplace is a worker who has been a dedicated employee but despite following all the rules is passed over a desired promotion because of office politics.

- The gap between what is expected versus what one gets is experienced as a disappointment. The disappointment of missed expectations results is experienced as frustrated aggression known as stress. Associated missed expectations such as the worker feeling trapped having no viable alternatives compounds the intensity of stress.

How Stress Feels

In describing how stress feels a person will often describe him or herself as being attacked by forces they can't control. Additionally there is a sense that this is not at all how the course of one's life should have been written.

Those who are stressed typically are weighted down by feelings including victims of a conspiracy, self-pity (why me), pessimism, raw fury, powerlessness, helplessness, hopelessness, detachment, and numbness.

Causes of Stress

People like to maximize pleasure and minimize pain. This is called the pleasure principle. The pleasure principle dominates childhood thinking as well as adults who have found it difficult to acknowledge and cope with inevitable life limitations (the reality principle.)

Much of what happens in life can be described as coming to terms with a never-ending conflict between the pleasure principle and the reality principle.

The formula for the pleasure principle is: I want what I want when I want it meaning all my desires should be instantly gratified — no frustration allowed.

When the formula appears to be working I feel totally in control of my life and feel I and my life are "perfect". I conclude this is the way my life and reality should be.

By contrast, if and when my desires are blocked either by myself or some external source then by definition I will experience a gap between what should be versus what is. I will experience this gap between wish and reality as a disappointment. Disappointment (frustrated aggression due to a missed expectation) is further experienced as unpleasant tension commonly referred to as stress.

We all can identify with the above. There are countless times during any given day when we fail to get what we want in a timely fashion. Thus we all encounter frequent disappointments experienced as frustration. But the quality and intensity of the frustration differs to the degree of the space between what we have versus what we want to get.

A little bit of space between what is actual from what is ideal is experienced as a small degree of frustration. A large gap between what is real versus what should be real is experienced as a greater degree.

Some Symptoms Associated With Stress

Symptoms of stress include:

(1) Physical symptoms, such as headache and fatigue

(2) Mental symptoms, such as poor concentration

(3) Emotional symptoms, such as irritability and depression.

(4) Social symptoms, such as isolation and resentment [Mayo Clinic]

A Representative composite list of symptoms associated with stress, and anxiety include:

Shock, denial, hyper hypo emotionality, exhaustion, excessive energy, fatigue, anxiety, panic, depression, despair, catastrophe, anxiety/fear, guardedness, suspicion, need for atonement, a greater sense of humanity, a wish to be rescued, a wish to go to bed and pull the covers up over our heads, anger, need for revenge, guilt, survival guilt, uncertainty anxiety, vulnerability, easily distracted, a need to be with people, confusion, fear of the unknown, generalized insecurity, vulnerability, sadness, grief, detachment, guilt, disappointment, bewilderment, frustration, abandonment fears, and abandonment anxiety, ambiguity, complexity, death fears and death anxiety, obsessing, generalized insecurity, and desperation.

Low and High Levels of Stress

An example of a relatively low level of stress is, wanting to purchase the favorite toy of the year for your child only to discover that the last one was sold out just as you asked for it. A higher level of stress is likely to be experienced when you have to wait on the results of a biopsy with the realistic possibility that the results indicate you have stage three cancer.

Both 'gaps' [between desired outcome and actual reality] may be experienced as stressful. That which determines the felt degree of tension is the relative meaning people attribute to the 'gap' in question.

In both examples what you want, and when you want it are largely out of your control. It almost doesn't matter what your feelings are about it as the outcome will be independent of your wishes.

No matter what the tension is associated with – management of stress ultimately means that you have to be able to bear whatever the degree of intensity is at the moment, so that you can remain steady under pressure functioning as well as you can.

The key to effectively managing stress is the increasing capacity to tolerate inevitable frustration.

To do this requires a person to change their attitude about frustration, which is comprehensively dealt with in detail as you continue to read the rest of Attitude Shifting™.

What Is Anxiety?

Anxiety is the subjective feeling of dread whenever a person believes that they are in the presence of a real or imagined danger threatening the integrity of the self. It functions as an early warning signal energizing the system for self protection taking the form of fight or flight. Thus is it like a siren or hurricane report warning people to adequately prepare to protect themselves.

Anxiety ranges on a continuous line from a relatively low level (i.e. existential anxiety) to break the bank i.e. panic or catastrophe anxiety.

What Causes Anxiety

We re-iterate ...Contrary to what many of the drug companies would have us believe anxiety (or depression, or frustration) is not pathological. They are inevitable and unavoidable natural reactions to the normal stresses and strains of daily living.

Anxiety is the feeling that is experienced when adrenalin is released from the primitive brain and flows into autonomic nervous system. Adrenalin is released when a person experiences a real or imagined threat to the integrity of the self.

Adrenalin energizes the system for potential fight or flight. All mammals are capable of becoming anxious. Human beings are mammals. Although anxiety feels 'bad' it is actually good that we have this capacity. If we did not we could not instinctually protect ourselves in the midst of realistic threats.

It is noteworthy that adrenalin is neutral. When it is released in the body it may be experienced as one or a combination of the following three feelings: fear, anxiety, and or excitement.

An apt example of all three is the fact that human beings spend millions of dollars each year on rides which only last a few minutes at a carnival for the purposes of shaking them up.

What determines whether the adrenalin is experienced as fear, anxiety, or excitement depends on the meaning a given person assigns to the context in which these feelings are experienced.

These distinctions are important as the management of anxiety and other painful affects (including frustration, and stress) require different interventions in order to effectively cope with them. It should be noted that the effectively coping with anxiety and stress depends on how complicated a person is with respect to their total psychology (psychodynamics).

Just as some machines are relatively simple in having few components that interact, others are extraordinarily intricate in design and interactions.

When a perceived threat to the integrity of the human system is real then the adrenalin is experienced as fear. When the threat to the integrity of the system is imagined, the adrenalin is referred to as anxiety. Sometimes there is a combination of the two.

Imagine crossing a street and seeing an out of control car heading straight for you. Instinctually the autonomic nervous system releases adrenalin into the system creating a shock to the system (fear) to mobilize the system to remain frozen or run like hell to avoid the anticipated crash. Now imagine the same conditions. Except this time when it seems like a car is out of control threatening to hit you — you correctly observe there is no car at all — in fact there are no traffic at all.

Clearly, in this case, your imagination is working overtime. But you still have the released adrenalin flowing into your system warning you that there is some sort of threat from which you had better take steps to protect yourself.

In this case — since there is no 'real' threat then you have to locate the source of the imagined out of control car hurtling down on you coming from your memory.

In my work as a psychoanalyst both personally and professionally virtually every anxiety attack, when analyzed (broken down to its components) can be traced to a traumatic occurrence in the history of the patient in question that has not been sufficiently put to rest.

This means that something in the here and now has somehow connected with and stirred up an unresolved psychological problem from the persons past.

All anxiety attacks have a potentially identifiable trigger, which is associated in the context of a given person's life in the last 24 to 48 hours.

Differentiating Anxiety from Fear

It is important to take note that the anxiety and fear are commonly used interchangeably. This is important, as there are significant differences that potentially affect the outcome in a potential responder's effectiveness or lack of effectiveness in helping a person suffering from fear and or anxiety.

The difference between fear and anxiety is that fear is the experience of a real present threat to the integrity of the self whereas anxiety is the experience of an imaginary threat to the integrity of the self having its origins in the person's past.

Technically fear is the warning sign that a real — not imagined — threat is imminent. An example is crossing a street and seeing an out of control truck speeding in your direction. Fear warns the self to run as fast as you can to avoid potential destruction to life and limb.

If the same person crossing the street perceives a truck hurtling towards them but upon careful looking is aware there is no real out of control truck — only an imaginary one — then the same warning signal is called anxiety — not fear.

Both anxiety and fear are contagious. In the presence of someone who is experiencing anxiety it is often difficult not to get caught up in the invisible waves of intense feeling that anxiety radiates. This means those who are trying to help people cope with anxiety must make ego boundaries between themselves and those in need of help.

For example when in the presence of a person overwhelmed with panic anxiety it is difficult not to feel as nervous as they are (a process of over-identification). While this would be a good thing for the helper to have empathy for the panicked person it would not be helpful for either one to experience the same panic anxiety.

The helper is most helpful when he/she can empathize with the pain of the person in need of help but at the same time remain relatively neutral or objective.

The origin of the threat of danger from one's past experienced as anxiety in the person's present is a conscious or unconscious memory of a traumatic occurrence that actually did happen in the person's past that has been revived in the present.

In the example of the person imagining that a truck was threatening their existence might be the revival of a past event when the person was either in an accident or witnessed one and the memory of what it felt like and meant was never fully processed at the time.

These distinctions are important as the management of anxiety and other painful affects (including frustration, and stress) require different methods to effectively cope with them. It should be noted that effectively coping with anxiety and stress depends on how complicated a person is with respect to their total psychology (psychodynamics).

Just as some machines are relatively simple in having few components that interact, others are extraordinarily intricate in design and interactions.

DEPRESSION

In addition to anxiety and stress a common complaint of a person in the throes of an emotional crisis is their experience of what they describe as overwhelming depression.

What is Depression?

Whereas anxiety is associated with some anticipated future pain, depression is associated with some loss that in the past of the person was experienced as pleasurable.

Depression feels depressing as if; one were weighted down by some heavy force pinning the person to the ground.

Symptoms Associated With Depression

- An all pervasive sense of sadness
- Overwhelmed by feeling stuck in negative inertia
- Passivity
- Helplessness
- Hopelessness
- Extreme pessimism
- Drained

The Causes of Depression

There are both physiological and psychological causes of depression. Physiological causes of depression are a chemical imbalance. Psychological causes of depression are the experience of some valued person, place, thing, idea, that is 'lost.'

Thus, the hope of a talented runner eventually becoming an Olympian who crushes his legs, may likely result in an overwhelming depressive reaction.

Another cause of psychological depression is the result of anger (aggression) turned into the self.

The objects of loss associated with depression are experienced as if someone important died.

How They Affect Us

Anxiety is associated with the future in that it anticipates some potential ill occurrence.

Depression is associated with the person's past triggered off by the experience of a valued something lost.

Stress is present time in which a person feels frustrated feeling unable to close the gap between what one has versus what one wants to have.

Each of these feelings is triggered by some external and or internal event. The triggering event whether internal or external is called a stressor.

In my work as a psychoanalyst both personally and professionally, virtually every anxiety attack, when analyzed (broken down to its components) can be traced to a traumatic occurrence in the history of the patient in question that has not been sufficiently put to rest.

Whether it is stress, anxiety or a combination of the two – in every case these painful feelings are triggered by a combination of an external stressor event and some internal meaning assigned to it.

This means that something in the here and now has somehow connected with and stirred up an unresolved psychological problem from the persons past.

Practical and Psychological Triggers

Whether anxiety, depression, or stress, each is triggered by a response to either: (1) some external surface issue (problem) which is initially felt to be unsolvable, and/or to (2) some internal stressor.

An example of an external practical surface stressor event is Joe having to manage an avalanche of a combination of surface issues. These include: Joe's car literally being stuck in the mud, the loss of his job; his fear of breaking down; his fear of his wife's probable negative reaction when he tells her his bad news and so forth.

By internal we mean the trigger event is located in the person's inner reality.

Internal Stressors

Not all stress stems from things that happen to you, some of the stress response can be self-induced. Those feelings and thoughts that pop into your head and cause you unrest are known as internal stressors

Examples of internal stressors include:

Fears

These can be things such as the fear of flying, heights or more subtle apprehensions like speaking to a group of strangers or meeting people at a party.

Uncertainty

Stemming perhaps from a looming restructuring at the office or waiting for medical test results.

Pessimism

Having a negative view of the world in and of itself can be stressful, since you create an unpleasant environment in which to live.

Unrealistic Expectations

A perfectionist or controlling personality may lead to unnecessarily high stress levels. Over-scheduling and not planning ahead can lead to a world of worries.

Blurred ego boundaries

Time Boundaries: Confusing clock time (past, present, future) with durational or vacation time (timelessness).

Space Boundaries: Confusing inner reality feelings with external reality facts.

These can be things such as the fear of flying or heights, or more subtle apprehensions like speaking to a group of strangers at a party.

Contents of Consciousness Boundaries

Unable to distinguish thoughts, feelings, intuitions, and bodily sensations.

Trigger Events

Are Those That Upset a Persons' usual Expectations of Cause and Effect.

The following lists commonly held assumptions that when challenged often lead to triggering anxiety, depression and or stress:

The loss of any pet conscious and unconscious organizing concept – i.e. the illusion of a mantle of protection; God will always protect me; I am invincible

- ✓ The illusion of absolute certainty
- ✓ All problems are resolvable
- ✓ Love conquers all
- ✓ Wishing makes it so – the stronger the wishing the more likely the wish will be fulfilled.

Armed with the knowledge that whether a person is experiencing fear, anxiety or excitement and that these are three reactions to the experience of adrenalin we have a potentially important weapon in understanding how to effectively treat patients who are complaining about stress, anxiety and frustration.

Choice and Change-There is a Difference

The first step toward assisting in stress relief is to realize where the stress is coming from. Your stress (emotional pain) is an allergic reaction to one basic toxic belief with two components:

(1) Others have to change because they have caused my suffering (stress); and/or

(2) I have to change because I am responsible for other's thoughts, feeling and actions."

Relief of stress begins when you stop trying to change others and instead concentrate on making choices to get what you want.

The Difference between Choice and Change

No one can make you feel anything. Feelings are individual reactions to internal and external triggers (stimuli). People vary with respect to how they experience the same trigger.

Note: Twin brothers both describe their father as being tyrannical, loud, and threatening. In the presence of the father when worked up cowers in fear; whereas the other brother laughs and sticks out his tongue.

For our purposes it is apt to conclude that brother one is choosing to cower, whereas brother two pushes back.

Although brother one is reacting with fear to a perceived threat, theoretically he might learn how to choose a different attitude such as pushing back like his twin brother.

In assuming responsibility for your actions and reactions you set the stage for choosing to change your attitudes to whatever triggers you encounter. In so doing "you become the primary creative force in your life. Because your choices create your experiences, you can create the experiences you want by making new choices.

<u>Choice is easy. The only energy you need is to be aware of what current options you have to select from.</u>

This Attitude Shifting™ Guide acquaints the first responder and the stressed with realistic options to enable them to move from passive stuckness to active momentum.

Attitude Shifting™

Joe's Story

In this light we invite you to read Joe's compelling story - a representative anecdotal multi leveled stressful situation derived from from today's economic upheaval… and his CHOICES.

Joe, who has been working as a machinist for the last 20 years, is told that because of the economic downturn his company is going out of business, which means, he'll be out of a job in one month. His first reaction to this unexpected news is to freeze. After his shock lifts, his next reaction is facing his stark reality. As he has no other marketable skills, and the location he is working in is in a deep recession, the odds of hid quickly finding another position with equal benefits is remote.

Adding to his troubles is the fact that his 10 year old daughter needs surgery but because of a no pre existing condition clause on his insurance plan he will have to pay for it on his own. As the family has meager savings, and there are no relatives capable of financially helping out, his stress deepens.

Compounding an already burdensome situation is his dread of telling his wife the bad news as she has been worrying about how they will pay the extra expenses for their daughters' care, as well as having to manage additional stress in taking care of a sickly and demanding parent.

Characteristic of Joe's style, he initially absorbs the bad news like a professional prize fighter being punched in the ring. Proud of his "M O" to reliably rise to the occasion, he has been judged by himself and others to be a strong man who faces his troubles with resolve, determination and a generally optimistic outlook.

Girding up, as if he was a soldier heading into battle, Joe gets in his car, and heads home to tell his wife the bad news. Half way, exhausted from worry, he pulls over to the side of the road to take a nap.

On awakening he becomes aware that during his nap there has been a downpour. Attempting to resume his trip, Joe realizes he is stuck in the mud. Utterly frustrated and angry he guns the motor.

Adding insult to injury, he experiences the car's spinning wheels parallel to his spinning feelings — both himself and the car sinking into the mud going nowhere fast, feeling overwhelmingly stuck.

Like every human being, Joe has his personal breaking point and with this last unexpected frustration he reaches the tipping point of his endurance. Unable to move forward, he experiences a rush of intense frustration, panic anxiety, helplessness, hopelessness, confusion, bewilderment, and intense anger leaving him feeling overwhelmed.

This convergence of negative feelings is bad enough, but worse is the fact that Joe is not used to feeling vulnerable. Upon entering his home, feeling shaky and insecure, he makes a beeline for the couch, slumping down into the cushions.

Attempting to calm himself, he turns on the radio to get some needed comfort in listening to his favorite music station, but, instead hears an ad for A GREAT REMEDY.

Turning the dial, Joe hears one ad after another offering the same advice as to how to get relief from anxiety, depression, and stress. Resonating to the content, he can't help but feel that these ads are talking directly to him.

His attention now focused, the content of the ads essentially deliver the same message — that anxiety, depression, and stress are painful feelings that can be relieved by taking the newest drug of the moment.

The ads further declare that the cause of these implied 'pathological' feelings is due to a "chemical imbalance." <u>Or is it?</u>

Then, they logically reason that since Joe's distressful unbalanced state is assumed to be caused by a chemical imbalance the obvious 'cure' in restoring his lost balance is for him to try popping the 'just right' pill.

The ads advise Joe that the best way for him to follow up is to remember the name of the drug in the ad, then call his doctor as soon as possible, being sure to mention the name of the drug, implying that the Doctor will probably have him come in for an appointment and give him a prescription. And if his doctor does not feel competent to prescribe medication for his symptoms then he is likely to send Joe to a psychiatrist who probably will.

At first hearing, realizing he needs help, Joe is tempted to follow the ads advice. In the midst of a convergence of multiple problems and feeling stressed out as a reaction to them, the idea of simply 'popping a pill' with its promise of scientific relief seems reasonable and compelling enough.

Except for the fact that ... listening very carefully with heightened attention, Joe realizes that at the end of each advertisement is a long list of potentially harmful side effects which disturbs his brief calm causing him to wonder if the cure is potentially worse than the disease.

Echoing his realistic concerns, in discussing his feelings with his wife, she tells him about her best friend who has been on anti depressants and anti anxiety medication for the past year.

The friends' experience is a mixed review. While true she has not felt as depressed or anxious since she's been taking pills, at the same time she is bitter about putting on an unexpected twenty pounds making her feel old and fat, worsened by her belief that the medication has destroyed her sex life. Hearing these details makes Joe's heart beat faster intensifying his doubts and confusion.

Desperate for relief, but uncertain as to what he should do, Joe alternates between choosing to call his doctor versus toughing it out. He realizes he's near his breaking point but wants to make an informed decision.

He knows he needs help but has doubts about the drug ad's mixed messages. He now finds himself with an escalating intensification of painful feelings with no clear-cut path to relieve them. While the drug ads are seductive he goes to bed worrying they might do him more harm than good.

He needs to manage his stress but is feeling too overwhelmed, stuck, and helpless to take action. He feels drained as if his motor was running on fumes.

Does Joe have any options left? He clearly needs some external help but his family is as drained as himself. Where might Joe and his family seek appropriate help? Might the answer in part possibly be you?

Attitude Shifting™

ARE YOU YOUR BROTHER'S KEEPER?
SHOULD YOU BE YOUR BROTHER'S KEEPER?
HOW TO BE YOUR BROTHER'S KEEPER!

The Need for a Helper

Having exhausted his resources to manage his stress by himself Joe must either seek appropriate external help, or at least be open to responding to some caring person's offer to be helpful.

Whether you are an intimate friend or even just a caring stranger sensing that Joe needs help – is there anything you can do?

What we usually do is:
Observe and continue on with our own agenda, while those in need of help usually continue to do any one or more of the following: deny, become more frightened, lounge in their fears and frustrations, complain, worry, strike out, over indulge in drinking, smoking or eating etc., mask the pain, implode, explode, endlessly obsess and worry while sinking ever deeper into negative inertia.

Once aware ... A Helper chooses to reach out.

To be clear that we are all on the same page it is valuable to describe the multiple dimensions of the potentially effective helper.

These dimensions include: the definition of a helper; who is a helper; the role of the helper; attitudes of an effective helper; and steps in becoming an effective helper.

The Helper Defined

In our everyday lives we almost everyday encounter situations where we personally have developed stressful situations or we meet someone who has developed a stressful situation.

A helper is one who has become aware of someone you believe to be under stress and requiring some compassionate understanding.

Who is a Helper?

- First Responders
- Professionals
- Teachers
- Nurses
- Parents
- Police
- Judges
- Virtually any one who wishes to lend a helping hand.

The Role of the Helper

Helpers are faced with:

✓ People flooded with intense anxiety and stressed out
✓ People who are experiencing a sense of urgency
✓ A war atmosphere — emergency conditions
✓ On the front lines of war like atmospheres forced to act decisively
✓ People with an urgent need to experience instantaneous relief of the pain of their symptoms
✓ People who wish to be rescued or at least guided
✓ People who wish to be taken by the hand and then concretely shown what to do and how to do it.

Attitudes of the Effective Helper

Note: To be an effective helper you MUST show as many of these attitudes as possible:

- ✓ Engaging
- ✓ Empathic
- ✓ Active
- ✓ Authentic
- ✓ Caring
- ✓ Unconditionally accepting
- ✓ Non Judgmental
- ✓ Carefully listening to detail
- ✓ Trustworthy
- ✓ Firmly flexible
- ✓ Well Informed
- ✓ Armed with good organizing concept

Note: The overall task of the effective helper is to initiate a discovery process with people in need of help.

Steps in Becoming an Effective Helper

For the purposes of this guide let's stay with Joe who is stressed out. Joe is representative of the kind of person we identify as being in need of help.

A number of formidable issues have converged triggering off an overwhelming mixture of anxiety, depression, and immobilizing frustration. Joe's usual resilience to cope with his stress is close to the breaking point. Feeling quintessentially stuck Joe and his equally overwhelmed family members, clearly need some external help.

It is in this context that a sensitive caring neighbor, relative, good friend or even a sensitive observer aware of Joe's distress might be just the potential helper Joe – and his family – desperately need in helping them to manage their stress.

Attitude Shifting™

When They Need More Than Just A Friend

Getting "under the material" assumes that for every individual there is an internal reality (personal subjective reality) separate from external reality (consensually validated reality).

While for many people this idea of a personal internal reality separate from an external reality is a no brainer for many others it is a novel and indeed somewhat shocking [good shocking] experience. This is especially so when a person experiences it for the first time.

Whereas all people are different, they often present common complaints which signal the need for effective crisis intervention. A representative description of those in need of in depth consultation (Crises Intervention) is the following:

<u>CASE</u>: Adam complains about feeling lost and confused. He feels as if he has been going round and round in circles going nowhere fast. He is aware of intense states of anxiety, frustration and depression.

Anti anxiety medication does take off the edge but he feels that he is just masking what really should be attended to but he doesn't know what else to do. He feels as if his life is filled with gaps as he moves episodically from one experience to another with no sense of continuity.

During the times when he is in touch with him self he can't seem to hold on to it, feeling as if he literally loses himself. He believes he has to somehow get underneath his material but lacks knowhow as to how to go about doing this.

All attempts to deal with these symptoms are experienced as inadequate as they bring only short term relief. **Attitude Shifting**™ assumes that the reason for limited success in coping with their problems is that they are concentrating mainly on symptom reduction rather than on identifying underlying causes.

Engaging a Person in Need of Help

People in a state of crisis want immediate relief (that is to reduce the psychological pain associated with a given internal or external stressor.) The main 'weapons' the first responder has are his authentic desire to extend a caring hand, his/her natural 'bed side manner', and the enlightening concepts and psychological 'tools' he chooses to employ in a given intervention.

The first responder will convey both his attitude of genuine caring as well as transmitting his powerful concepts and psychological tools by communicating special words.

The dispensing of genuine care is what is meant by a positive 'bed side' manner. I know for a fact that just a little bit of genuine care administered by a genuinely caring person can go along way to helping the person overwhelmed with negative feelings to regain their lost sense of balance (their sense of 'normal'.)

"As a practicing psychoanalyst for the past 44 years, who, is also an expert in crisis intervention, I have repeatedly witnessed even the most frightened, depressed, stressed out patients regain their composure upon leaving the first session with a sense of hope and spirits lifted as a direct result of accepting them unconditionally, carefully listening to every word, being empathic, and offering some encouragement, illuminating concepts, and psychological tool (s) to be used by them for the purposes of empowerment."

Attitude Shifting™

The Discovery Process

Once a person in need of help is engaged, the responder initiates the following 5 step process.

Step 1- Discovering the Surface Issue in every crisis

Step 2- Moving the focus of the person from a preoccupation with the external surface trigger issue to identifying his/her internal emotional responses

Step 3- Identifying the person's attitudes towards his emotional responses

Step 4- Educating the person to his need to shift his negative attitudes to positive

Step 5- Suggesting specific Exercises (Attitude Shifters™) enabling a person to shift his initial negative attitudes to positive.

Implementing the Discovery Process

Observing their apparent states of stress.

The Case of John

> You come home and are immediately aware that your 15 year old son is looking glum, withdrawn, and obviously upset. You know this is out of character because he is usually upbeat and engaging.
>
> You know he is hurting and would like to help but also don't want him to feel you are invading his privacy.

Question: "What can you do?"
Answer: Ask discovery questions.

By making observations about people that feel out of control and helpful, you enter their reality of themselves and become a part of their reality. Once you are a part of their reality, you can then impact their reality.

Additionally, one of the most effective ways of eliciting the state that people are in is to ask very specific questions; in fact, the more specific the question, the higher the quality of information you'll get back.

Initial Discovery Questions

One or more and or a variant of these questions is a useful way to engage the person in need of help.

- Engaging the person in need of help by asking "You look stressed and anxious. Would you like to tell me about it?"
- Assess the issues by asking: "You look like you are either going to implode or explode. Can I Help?"

"What is your biggest CONCERN today?"

"Have you ever been helped with these type of feelings before"?

If yes —"Did it relieve your pain? What worked?"

If no —"What didn't work?"

Further Discovery Questions

1. Have you ever been stressed like this before?
2. Tell me about that (those) episodes
3. What triggered them?
4. How long did they last?
5. What did you do to relieve the stress?
6. What do you think triggered the episode?
7. Go Over the list of 'Triggers'

To add to your discovery of their issues and what people are thinking is to draw them out.

Some good examples are statements like these, which will work to pull people out in virtually any situation and help you garner their trust by seeming to be very insightful:

"You appear to me to be a person who is an independent thinker and doesn't accept others' opinions without strong evidence of truth."

"At the end of the day, it seems like you have a great deal of unused capacity that is going to be channeled into something even more meaningful and creative."

"You prefer a little change and variety, and when corralled by restrictions, limitations, or small thinking, you become dissatisfied."

But, first you must understand the difference between Choice and Change when considering the effects of changing an Attitude. Pay careful attention to the first responses stressed people make. They will quickly indicate their relative openness or closedness for further discussion. If open proceed to the next section of this guide which is implementing the 5 step process we call Attitude Shifting™.

*My experience indicates that more often than not - **refusing to give up on the person needing help** – is experienced by them as you caring often resulting in their being receptive to your help*

Having engaged a person in need of help, the potentially effective helper initiates a process of discovery essential in an effective crisis intervention we refer to as Attitude Shifting™.

Step 1 - Discovering the Surface Issue in every crisis

It is characteristic of most people to believe that the cause of their stress (in whatever form such as panic anxiety, depression, and debilitating frustration) is due to one or more surface, external issues. Such issues include Joe's having to face that in one month he is losing his job.

The following is a list of 17 typical surface external issues associated with these trigger events are often thought of as psychological stressors often experienced as overwhelming anxiety, depression, frustration, and or stress. triggering crisis situations.

Money, Money, Money

Due to the recession my patient work load has been dropping. I have used up my IRA and am now in severe debt.

I haven't paid the IRA taxes for the last 6 months. I am afraid they are going to throw me in jail.

The bank is threatening to foreclose our mortgage, which hasn't been paid in over three months. I worry all day we will be thrown out of our home any day. I feel sick and weak.

Just Plain Pressured

My wife says I am up tight all the time. I am negative, quick to pick fights, yell at the kids for minor infractions, and feel sullen and low.

I used to love each new day. Now I hate getting up. I feel sick to my stomach when I get within 100 feet of my office. I feel as if I am in a war manning a machine gun all night long. I wish a helicopter would pick me up and send me for a prolonged rest.

I am sick and tired of just getting by coping with pain. I would like to have more pleasure and excitement but everything I see looks dark.

My Job is a Pain in the A...

Feeling like screaming, 'I hate my job!' as the alarm goes off? Working a job you hate can be stressful.

In the last year my company of 1000 workers has had three major layoffs. Although I have been told numerous times my job is secure I am worried it will happen to me.

My boss is a sadist who rules with fear. I cringe in his presence. I also feel my tension increasing and scared of either being bullied by him or exploding and getting fired.

I'm not Going to Take it Anymore

I have tried out practically every self help exercises with the hope of getting rid of or at least reducing my stress. At best the initial positive results only last for a short period of time. It stresses me out that I can't seem to find a long lasting way to cope with it.

I have been advised to go into long term psychotherapy but I am skeptical of investing a lot of time and money into treatment which may not work. I have read numerous self help books but they all seem to be superficial or assume I am more capable of changing on my own which I know I am not.

I have figured out that the core of my chronic distress seems to be an aversion to feelings of frustration, anxiety, depression, and tension. I hate all of them but am aware there is nothing I can do to get rid of them.

I am a highly experienced and competent care giver but recently feel as if I don't want to help anymore. I seem to have lost my professional objectivity.

Time Isn't What it Used to Be

I find myself constantly busy, always on edge, wishing I had more leisure time, and feeling overwhelmed by internal and external forces. I find it almost impossible to live in the moment and am constantly reliving some past loss or anticipating some feared future event.

The Importance of Staying Healthy

I had major bypass surgery 6 months ago which the Doctors say was successful. But since it happened I am worried that it can happen again.

This thought stresses me out and makes me feel anxious. When I feel anxious I worry that the pain is a signal that I may be on the verge of another heart attack.

The increasing reports of e-coli, listeria, bird flu and other disease epidemics, is scarring the hell out of me.

I am afraid to go to sleep because I know I will have nightmares, which feel absolutely real.

Who Am I Really?

I was wired to be super sensitive to noise, bright lights and being touched which is bad enough. However I have also had 6 operations on my right foot and am scheduled for another in two months.

I feel bitter, deeply frustrated, and all but totally hopeless unable to do even the simplest of activities. It is a victory for me to just get up every morning and brush my teeth.

I was coasting along feeling as if everything was in and under my control. However in the last few months I lost my job, my husband is having an affair, my kids are both having trouble at school. I feel like a total failure as a person, a wife, and as mother.

Most of my friends seem to know exactly who they are and what they should do to have a good life. Unfortunately I feel lost, confused, and feel as if I am going round and round in circles without a clear sense of purpose and direction.

I am a psychologist in private practice for the last 20 years. My anal should have mastered these kinds of feelings. Just died and I feel as if I am scared to death.

Major Life Changes

We have lived in our home for thirty years loving every minute of it. But due to a foreclosure we are forced to move in 60 days. My family are scared to death bursting out in tears almost paralyzed.

Environmental Issues

Despite denials to the contrary by the local gas drillers that 'fracking' is perfectly safe, we are afraid to drink the tap water.

Unpredictable Events Issues

During the last severe weather event we lost everything. It is difficult to get out of bed. It is hard to hold on.

Social Issues

I am severely shy and self-conscious. I feel as if an invisible biographer is following me around writing down every wrong thing I am doing.

War Is Hell

I am an injured vet who had an intake interview with the VA. They gave me a diagnosis of PTSD and a date for counseling in a month. I am very feel overwhelmed, and not sure I can hold out till then. Is there anything I can do for myself?

If I Could Only Stop!

I have been in treatment for heroin addiction four different times. I am able to control myself in a structured program. But each time I leave a program I get hooked again. Is there anything I can do to help myself stay clean?

My Weight Is Killing Me

Due to medication changing my metabolism I have gained 40 pounds. I look ugly and I feel literally weighted down. I cry every time I look into a mirror and feel like climbing into my bed and pulling the covers over my head.

Death and Dying Issues

There have been a run of deaths of friends I was close to in High School. I can't get the thought of my head that if it happened to each of them it can happen to me. Now I worry all the time when is it my turn?

Marital

Last night my wife informed me that she had consulted with a divorce lawyer. This morning I was unable to get out of bed.

I love my wife but find that we are arguing too much. Attempts at marriage counseling have failed. I don't like feeling negative but that seems to be the basic reality.

Sexual Issues

I get nervous and tense just thinking about having sex.

My wife has been receiving infertility shots every month. I am more than willing to undergo the expense but find myself unable to perform.

Children

Until last year when my son was 12 we always had a great relationship. Now he seems to want to have nothing to do with me. He goes into his room, shuts the door, saying I embarrass him.

I have read that this is normal for a boy of his age. However it has evoked very strong negative feelings about him even to the point of my regretting I ever got my wife pregnant. I feel ashamed and guilt for having thoughts and feelings like this.

Any half way sensitive human being knows only too well how these existential surface issues can and often do happen when we least expect them and are inevitable life problems, which require priority attention.

We also know that a practical resolution of any of these surface problems is often daunting at best with good resolutions escaping our immediate grasp.

Apt solutions to any or all of them generally require adequate time to think through various options. Effective resolutions are often incremental and rarely instantaneous.

So while we would all like to be magicians and solve 'the problems of the world' by waving a magic wand we know this is a child's fantasy and that as adults we have no other alternative than to face up to the daunting problem of the moment and dig in for the long pull.

This is a mature and healthy attitude to facing the immediacy of a seemingly unsolvable external stressor or combination of stressors.

Attitude Shifting™

But for many people the surface situation triggers emotional reactions, which switch the priority problem from the surface issue to a deeper internal emotional reaction to the surface problem.

This means that what is initially experienced as the primary problem now shifts to an internal problem namely managing what is initially experienced as overwhelming anxiety, depression, frustration and or stress.

Thus what is initially viewed as the primary problem (the external surface stressor) now becomes a symptom of a deeper, internal emotional problem requiring the immediate attention of the person and or a first responder engaged in helping the person in need of help.

It is often the case that people in need of help will complain about a number of issues each of which may trigger a combined emotional response experienced as anxiety, depression, frustration, and or stress.

Attitude Shifting™

It is helpful for the first responder to identify the various trigger situations with which the person in need of help is preoccupied.

Once having identified one or more trigger events (stressors) the first responder moves to step two of the discovery process: shifting the focus from the external surface to the internal emotional response.

Step 2: Shifting Your Focus

The first step toward assisting in stress relief is to realize where the stress is coming from - namely yourself. No person or situation in and of itself directly causes stress (or depression, frustration, anxiety); rather, it is the meaning and attitudes a person attributes to the external 'trigger' experience that results in stress.

A worker, like Joe, who panics when told he is going to be laid off, is likely to believe the cause of his stress is exclusively due to his pending lay off. In actuality, the cause of Joe's panic anxiety is not the bad news of the layoff in and of itself (a trigger event), but, is instead, Joe's attitude of catastrophe.

He attributes total disaster to his bad news resulting in his feeling overwhelmed with panic anxiety.

Attitude Shifting™

In general, people respond in their own unique ways to external stimuli even when such stimuli appear to be only negative.

This guide is written specifically for those people who initially respond to external stressors as if they are catastrophic.

Most of the literature on the subject of stress relief particularly of the self help genre offer a routine list of conventional exercises aimed at symptom relief. <u>The most popular</u>*:*

The next level of stress intervention is by many professionals who typically refer people in crisis to psychiatrists who are quick to prescribe medication instead of talk therapy. Implicitly they aim to reduce symptoms rather than to identify underlying causes.

The authors of this guide strongly believe that symptom relief alone is not sufficient enough to enable those in need of relief to feel significantly better.

Once having identified the emotional response of the person in need of help, the first responder turns to step three of the discovery process.

STEP 3: Identifying The Attitude of The Stressed

The first responder should ask the following:

- The first responder asks the "stressed" if he is able to identify what anxiety, depression, frustration, and or stress feels like to him or her.
- Once having identified what these feelings feel like the next task of the first responder is to identify the attitude that the "stressed" has for each and all of these 'negative' feelings.
- Would you please tell me your attitude or feelings about anxiety, frustration, depression, and stress?

Note: In practically every inquiry the first responder should not be surprised to hear the "stressed" to have a 'negative' attitude to anxiety, depression, frustration, and stress.

Typically the "stressed" will indicate that the experience of anxiety makes them feel anxious; depression results in more depression; frustration creates more frustration and stress causes more stress in a non ending repetitive looping.

Having identified a negative attitude to anxiety, depression, frustration, and stress the first responder moves to step four of the discovery process. Step four educates the 'stressed' with vitally important information that the key to effective long term management of these negative feelings depends on his/her shifting their negative attitude to positive towards anxiety, depression, frustration, and stress.

STEP 4 – The Need To Shift from A Negative Attitude to Positive

One factor that makes this guide unique is the rarely mentioned if at all fact that there has to be a shift in a person's attitude towards his emotional responses to the trigger event for effective long time mastery to occur. This shift necessitates a change in attitude from negative to positive with respect to experiencing anxiety, frustration, depression and or stress.

Attitude Shifting™

G.Williams says:

"This is so because I have witnessed that most people who come into their first psychotherapy session in a state of crisis when asked about their attitudes to anxiety, depression, frustration, and stress characteristically respond… "They get more anxious when they are anxious, more frustrated when they are frustrated, more depressed when they are depressed, and more stressed out when they are stressed."

Thus they typically hate these feelings experiencing them as attacked by invisible enemy 'forces' wishing they could instantly rid themselves of their painful discomfort, rather than confronting them head on viewing them as inevitable life limitations that have to be tolerated.

What the first responder has to try and communicate to the person in crisis, **contrary to the propaganda and misinformation often explicitly or implicitly disseminated by the pharmaceutical companies,** that feelings such as anxiety, frustration, depression, and stress are not pathological symptoms that should be suppressed or masked.

Each of them is a normal healthy reaction to inevitable life limitations.

Each of these normal reactions is necessary for our survival. They each signal that some active creative intervention is necessary to resolved inevitable complicated life problems to insure both basic survival as well as contributing to the creative process of forging and sustaining a life of meaningful significance (thriving).

It Works Like Magic!

This guide assumes that the core idea enabling the 'stressed' to effectively manage anxiety, depression, frustration and stress is to shift their negative attitudes to positive.

The question is asked: How does a person shift their attitude from negative to positive?

HOW ATTITUDES ARE SHIFTED from NEGATIVE to POSITIVE.

We believe that if you stay curious when encountering someone already with a stressed attitude you can begin to find out what their present attitude is and then lead them into trying a new approach.

To shift attitudes from negative to positive means that both the first responder and the stressed person are going to both be active participants in a shifting attitude process.

It is the task of the first responder to choose specific exercises believed to be those that are most relevant for the "stressed" person of the moment.

Once the "stressed" appears sufficiently motivated to change his attitude from negative to positive, the first responder moves to step 5 of the discovery process in which specific exercises are suggested.

Step 5 of the discovery process: Suggesting specific Exercises (Attitude Shifters™) enabling a person to shift his initial negative attitudes to positive.

Step five of the Discovery Process indicates that in order for significant change to happen the stressed will have to actively engage him or herself in carrying out exercises designed to shift their negative attitudes to positive.

As we have mentioned before, this guide assumes that the most effective way to master anxiety, frustration, depression, and stress is to identify underlying causes rather than just focus on reducing the pain associated with surface symptoms.

We have identified the cause of the symptoms of anxiety, frustration, depression, and stress as the negative attitude that most people who are overwhelmed by these symptoms reveal when asked to identify their attitudes towards them.

Changing attitudes from negative attitudes to positive not only results in relief due to the reduction of symptoms but, more importantly, provides the 'stressed' with the key to long term and permanent mastery of these negative feelings.

We want to emphasize that significant change can come about in even the most 'stressed' out people but there are no miracle. People change by initiating and sticking to a process consisting of selected exercises repeated until they have mastered the embedded task. The repetitions eventually become automatic responses.

In this connection some explanation is necessary to distinguish that what appears to be the surface external cause of stress is actually a symptom of an underlying internal cause.

For Example: The Case of Joe.

To effectively cope with his stress, Joe (our representative sample of a typically stressed out person) ultimately needs to change his negative attitude to positive with regards to his stress. Changing Joe's Attitude from What to What?

For Joe, the news of his pending layoff is initially experienced as a catastrophe taking the form of panic anxiety, depression, and overwhelming stress.

Once Joe has been engaged, step one of the discovery process aims to identify his primary issue not that of his pending job loss (the surface trigger situation/stressor) but redirecting his attention to his internal emotional responses of panic anxiety, depression, stress and additional 'negative' feelings.

While for many people this idea of a personal internal reality separate from an external reality is a no-brainer for many others it is a novel and indeed somewhat shocking [good shocking] experience. This is especially so when a person experiences it for the first time.

Attitude Shifting™

 WARNING!

The emphasis on words is a central assumption of this Guide.

This does not mean that the Helper should steer away from recommending a patient going to an emergency room of the nearest hospital, or to a psychiatrist for more intensive therapy, or being assessed for their possible need for drugs.

It does mean that if a stressed individual is first introduced to the potential power of special words experienced as therapeutic they may not require anything more than the intervention outlined in this guide.

The Helper must decide, as soon as possible, if empathy, understanding and a positive attitude to the responder's desire to help is notably creating an atmosphere of trust thereby reducing the symptoms of stress, or if not, deciding that he or she should recommend further professional help such as an immediate call to 911.

This guide has been created i.e. to provide specific exercises for those who wish to get underneath their material for potential long term relief and sustained mastery.

As we travel through the following pages we will refer you to the use of specific Attitude Shifters™ which you will utilize as psychological 'tools', enabling the person under stress to actively and effectively manage his/her painful feelings thereby **restoring a lost sense of balance and accompanying empowerment.**

Step 5: Identifying Specific Attitude Shifter Exercises

Once the core problem is identified [step 4] the helper' task is to suggest selected psychological tools (specific exercises) for the purpose of greatly reducing the intensity of the stresses' discomfort. We name these specific exercises Attitude Shifters™ aimed at providing quick and long lasting relief.

Practically all methods of coping utilize one or more exercises to reduce the negative effects of internal and external stressors. However, whereas each of the following exercises may be useful, not all of them will resonate equally with a given person at a given time. You, the responder, or the stressed individual will have to gauge which exercise(s) is potentially most helpful for them at a given time.

Wishing for the Perfect Exercise

The perfect exercise to sharply reduce the pain of anxiety, depression, frustration, and stress doesn't exist. If by perfection is meant the total long term elimination of the discomfort which accompanies these four painful feelings.

However there is one exercise that if tried is guaranteed to enable the sufferer to attain a surprisingly degree of immediate relief. The experience of this high degree of relief experienced as relaxation has an added benefit of providing essential hope to the sufferer that significant relief is possible thereby encouraging them to actively struggle with struggle to change their attitudes.

Attitude Shifting™

A Most Surprisingly Effective Exercise

TAKE A BATH or EXTENDED SHOWER

1. Fill a bathtub with water that has the just right temperature. Turn off the lights. Light some candles. Light up incense if you like it. Pour yourself a favorite drink. Put on some favorite music. Suit the lighting to the way you most like it.

2. Fill a bathtub with water that has the just right temperature. Turn off the lights. Light some candles. Light up incense if you like it. Pour yourself a favorite drink. Put on some favorite music. Suit the lighting to the way you most like it.

3. Blow up an inflatable bathroom pillow and fasten it on the tiles behind your head. Stay in the water for as long as you want to.

4. Having created a near perfect environment for yourself you are guaranteed to have an exquisitely satisfying feeling.

Although this exercise is a sure fire winner in producing the desired effects, it's positive effects are relatively short lasting. This is not a criticism. Short term relief instills hope that the painful conditions are able to change. But it is discouraging when the pleasurable relief shifts back to painful agony.

Conventional attempts to cope with anxiety, stress, depression, and frustration offer a multitude of exercises each of which works for some people. But their effects are generally short lived. For an extensive list of these approaches **see:** The List

We contend that the reason this exercise (as well as all of the conventional relaxation exercises listed further on) produce short term relief is due to the fact that they focus on relief of symptoms rather than confronting underlying causes.

Our research declares the underlying causes of the often intense pain associated with anxiety, depression, frustration, and stress is due to a negative attitude about each of these feelings-

"By shifting attitudes from negative to positive – short term symptom relief can be extended to long term mastery."

We contend that the reason this exercise (as well as all of the conventional relaxation exercises listed further on) produce short term relief is due to the fact that they focus on relief of symptoms rather than confronting underlying causes.

SPECIFIC ATTITUDE SHIFTERS

About the Use of Exercises

This is a formidable challenge for the potential helper or stressed thus you, the first responder, must do all you can to find an effective way to positively motivate the stressed to at least commit long enough to see if the process is truly helpful. People change by changing. Changing, in the present case, means the capability of anyone to change one's initial experience of frustration, anxiety, depression, and stress from negative to positive.

To change from negative to positive means to actively engage in a process which is designed to shift one's negative attitudes towards anxiety, depression, frustration and stress to positive.

Step 5 of the discovery process obligates the 'stressed' to actively participate in trying out the suggested exercises in the hope that he/she will experience for themselves that significant change (effective coping with these four negative feelings) is indeed possible.

A Pre Three Step Process

To ensure the probability of success in shifting negative to positive attitudes it is first necessary to activate a pre 3 step 5 process of intentions.

This process consists of:

    1-Accept not fight or deny your current reality including your being anxious, depressed, frustrated and or stressed.

    2- Make a choice to change your attitudes from negative to positive.

    3- Choose to actively participate in the exercises.

Thanks to: Gary Emery, Ph.D. and James Campbell, M.D.
From their book: Rapid Relief from Emotional Stress

APPLYING SPECIFIC ATTITUDE SHIFTERS™

It is to be born in mind that whatever the surface issue (the previously listed 17, perhaps there are more), each one only appears to be the priority issue associated with a crisis.

Instead, as has been noted, the real priority issue associated with a crisis is the attitude towards the negative feelings triggered by the 'stressed' response to the surface issue (stressor).

Thus what is typically thought to be the core problem – the surface issue – is in fact a symptom of a deeper psychological reaction to the problem; namely, an initial reaction of feeling overwhelmed by anxiety, depression, frustration and or stress.

This means that when the first responder in utilizing the discovery process, shifts the focus from the external surface event (stressor) – step 1 - to the internal reality (overwhelming emotional responses) step 2 – he objectively assesses what specific exercises (attitude shifters) are likely to be the most effective in any given situation.

There are essentially two groups of people in a state of stress who are differentiated with respect to their attitude to actively change: (1) an active positive group, and (2) a passive negative group.

Group one are accepting of the first responder's offer to lend a helping hand. They tend to be relatively open about their feelings, and are active participants in the discovery process. It generally takes little effort to motivate them to try the suggested exercise (attitude shifters).

For those in group one there is a single exercise that if carried out at least 15 minutes a day for a week should be enough to successfully shift their attitudes towards anxiety, frustration, and depression from negative to positive. This exercise follows:

EXERCISE -M1- IDENTIFYING YOUR ATTITUDES to Anxiety, Depression, Frustration, and Stress

Answer the question: "What is your attitude towards your anxiety, depression, frustration and / or stress?"

If, as expected, their attitudes towards these 'negative' feelings are also negative, the helper has to educate them to the fact that these feelings are normal, not pathological responses to realistic human limitations and therefore have to be mastered.

Having identified the person negative attitude, the next exercise is of particular use in providing a psychological tool for aiding the person to tolerate the negative feelings - a necessary step resulting in their being able to shift their attitudes from negative to positive.

Exercise – M2 – Learning to Bear Increasing Dosages of Frustration

(a) Find a place where you can be alone. Have a watch or clock with you.

(b) Identify the feelings of being stuck, or negative, or victimized, or as if you were a passive victim, and the associated feelings of caving into them.

(c) Now see how much time you can tolerate the painful feelings by timing your toleration quotient. Let's say you can endure 50 seconds on your first try.

(d) Now say to yourself that you know you can withstand at least 50 seconds of terrible feelings because you just did so and lived to tell the tale.

(e) Repeat this exercise pushing yourself to go beyond the 50 second mark. Let's say this time you can extend the toleration of your frustration/anxiety/depression/stress feelings for one minute and 40 seconds.

Attitude Shifting™

(f) Now run the experiment a third time pushing beyond your highest mark. Continuing to do this will enable you to discover a deceptively simple but profound secret.

The more you willing bear frustration / anxiety / stress the more they are able to bear subsequent frustration / anxiety / stress.

This exercise is like learning to high jump over a bar at let's say 4 feet. You begin with what you can do naturally and gradually up the rung a bit more so you struggle with the next challenge.

Successive graded successes will likely eventuate in your increasing capacity to achieve your goal of 4 feet. (A journey of a thousand miles begins with the first step.) Thus you learn to remain steady under pressure by small approximations to the goal).

This exercise is like learning to high jump over a bar at let's say 4 feet. You begin with what you can do naturally and gradually up the rung a bit more so you struggle with the next challenge.

Successive graded successes will likely eventuate in your increasing capacity to achieve your goal of 4 feet. (A journey of a thousand miles begins with the first step.) Thus you learn to remain steady under pressure by small approximations to the goal).

Being able to tolerate the painful states associated with anxiety, frustration, depression, and stress is a major accomplishment.

But there is even more that can realistically be done to further strengthen the capacity of everyone who conducts these exercises to become an effective problem solver.

Exercise M1 and M2 should result in a profound sense of empowerment. However these optimistic results do not always occur immediately. Why is this?

Although the participants may sound as if they are actively choosing to change the reality is that for them they aren't really connected to the experience of making choices. It is as if they simply passively follow directions rather than actively make an effort to struggle with struggle.

The next simple exercise is designed to enable people to actively connect with making choices.

EXERCISE – M3 - Experience making choices

Human beings take action all the time. Much of what we do is habitual such as walking to work the same way each day. The best way to become consciously aware of making choices is to do the following:

    (a) Before each action say to yourself I CHOOSE to whatever.

Examples: I choose to leave this room. I choose to cross this street. I choose to look in this shop. I choose to leave this shop immediately. I choose to walk to the right. I choose to walk to the left. I choose to walk forwards. I choose to walk backwards. I choose to stop. And so on…

    (b) This exercise should be done in 10 minute intervals throughout each day.

Attitude Shifting™

If conducted on a daily basis this exercise should result in significant feelings of empowerment in relatively short order.

Even if the person who is feeling anxious, accepts the need to make a choice to change, he or she may still hesitate in doing so. Why so?

Often the answer is because they are afraid to act. A fear of acting results in a person so frozen with anxiety rendering them from acting (acting on choices).

Actively choosing in this case means to actively participate in the discovery process by doing the suggested exercises (including this one.)

Even if a person is ready and willing to make choices to move from idea to attainment of a goal (making changes) a person has to complete the last step of this three part process by initiating action.

Because new experiences are by definition unfamiliar they will likely trigger anxiety (fear of the unknown). It is relatively easy to motivate a person to get ready then set which are the first two steps in the three-step process of making changes. However, it is not so simple to motivate a person who is fear ridden to make the final step - to act.

Since the odds are strong that even the most anxious person in the present situation has had similar occasions in the past and survived the worst of their fears this fact leads to exercise M4.

Exercise – M4 – **On Your Mark, Get Set, Go!**

Exercise 4 aims at encouraging a risk-averse person to face their fear of change with sufficient courage and determination so they can 'let go' and act.

If the present conflict is associated with some familiar conflict from his or her past, how did they feel about it, and what did they do to resolve it. What was learned?

Attitude Shifting™

The first responder instructs the 'stressed' to:

(a) Try recalling some times in the past when you faced your fears directly and courageously by getting ready, getting set and finally 'letting go?'

(b) For example: Imagine you are a relatively good diver but have been afraid to dive off the highest board. You would have liked to dive off the big board but every time for you to release your toes from the end of the board you got scared to death

If the present conflict is associated with some familiar conflict from his or her past, how did they feel about it, and what did they do to resolve it. What was learned?

The first responder instructs the 'stressed' to:

(a) Try recalling some times in the past when you faced your fears directly and courageously by getting ready, getting set and finally 'letting go?'

(b) For example: Imagine you are a relatively good diver but have been afraid to dive off the highest board. You would have liked to dive off the big board but every time for you to release your toes from the end of the board you got scared to death

Attitude Shifting™

*This principle is that the secret of changing is simple: you make a **CHOICE** to change [both facing and challenging your fear] and in so doing transform the passive idea of changing into an active action which is the externalization of changing.*

At these times it is often useful to request the stuck person to simply say whatever comes to his mind? If nothing is forth coming the person can be prompted with such questions as have you ever been stuck before? Did you feel the same way? What did you do to try to get over the stuckness?

With some stressed even though they wish to be helped act as if they can't tolerate 5 minutes delay to hear about what the first responder has on their mind.

These 'stressed' are grossly impatient. The following exercise is designed to enable such impatient people to learn how to be patient.

EXERCISE – M5 - **Learning how to be patient - (delaying action)**

The first responder says:

(a) Next few times you are stressed out try to identify the trigger event that leads to you feeling disappointed (missed expectation).

You might initially believe that the frustrated goal was something that should have been a snap to attain, but later to discover that it realistically required more time and effort to get it right?

(c) You might want to ask yourself why it is so important not to be disappointed or in a similar vein why can't you more gracefully give yourself repeated attempts to master the task at hand? What's the rush? Why can't you wait?

(d) Try considering negotiation and compromise as an alternative solution. That is in between either/or - is - and.

Or, another way to say the same thing is that even though an outcome seems to be a matter of do or die, all right or all wrong, all or nothing: there is in fact, a wide range of middle level possibilities.

These include:
- Most things can wait without dire circumstances happening
- All situations have mixtures and ratios of assets to liabilities
- Risk and rewards
-

There really is no such thing as perfection.

(e) Introduce the concept of degrees i.e. can conceptualize making changes as projecting a goal as the end point of a process (100%) which begins at a 0% starting point. There is a gap of 1 to 99 degrees.

(f) Progress in the attainment of a particular goal might be viewed in incremental advances. [0 to 5 degrees. Similarly 5 degrees to 33 degrees]

(g) The principle here is 'a journey of a thousand miles begins with the first step."

THE UNMOTIVATED

It is to be noted that different people will have different attitudes in their willingness to follow the suggestions of the helper.

It will soon become quite evident to the first responder or helper, how ready, willing, and able the "stressed" is insufficiently motivated to engage in the discovery process.

For example:

Despite their acceptance of the first responder's reaching out to them initially seem to be so 'resistant', stuck, innervated that makes them appear excessively unmotivated preventing them from getting any potential benefits utilizing this guide.

Experience indicates that even for these apparent 'unmotivated' stressed people the following exercises may help to transform them from being hopelessly stuck to actively engaging in struggling with their struggles.

Causes of a Lack of Motivation

Differences among those who are stressed have to do with such factors as their degree of felt stuckness, degrees of hope vs. hopelessness; and the degree of willingness to be an active participant versus being negatively passive.

Some reasons for the unmotivated sense of hopelessness and helplessness.

Resistance to being helped is due to many reasons. Among them is basic distrust, fear of being perceived as weak, needy, pitiable; fear of being criticized, belittled, judged; fear of being pushed around; low energy; feeling helpless, and hopeless.

When encountering people like Joe's friend who appear to be hopelessly unmotivated it is tempting to regard them as too 'resistant' and that it is best for all concerned to break off the contact.

Our experience indicates that it is exactly at this point when the first responder might be of the most potentially helpful.

For example: returning to Joe's friend, a caring and sensitive first responder might respond to the 'stressed' obvious resigned attitude saying:

"Look Joe's friend – your resignation is understandable as you feel intensely hopeless.

But I know from personal and professional experience what is critically important for you at this time is less you feelings of hopelessness than your attitude that your conviction that you are beyond help is absolutely true.

Your feelings no matter how strong they feel are not absolutely equal to the reality of possibilities.

"If you would borrow some of my optimism I would like you to try to carrying out one or more of our suggested exercises. I think you will pleasantly surprised."

Few people will resist, at least giving the exercises a try!

The principle here is to encourage the 'stressed' to simply get actively engaged. Engagement begins with the 'stressed' simply talking about anything at all.

It is apt to refer to these exercises as geared to those respondees who need to be positively motivated to commit themselves to changing their attitudes by embracing the mantra of struggling with struggle.

Exercises for the Un-Motivated

A core reason underlying a person's apparent lack of motivation in becoming actively engaged in the discovery process is one of an attitude of profound hopelessness. Therefore a need exists for an exercise that aims to have the 'stressed' create a sense of hope in the midst of a life filled with negativity.

EXERCISE -UM1- Creating hope in a life filled with negativity.

(a) Try recalling a memory or memories of the worst things you ever experienced.

(b)- Once having accessed similar emotionally parallel events from the past enables the person to recall what was experienced in the way of feelings, fantasies, thoughts and any predictions made with respect to future outcomes.

(c) Now speed up the 'projector' six months into the future. Ask yourself what actually happened? Were things in fact as bleak as you had predicted?

(d) Back in the present if you are able to recall what has happened and can accurately count the fingers on your hands you know you are alive having survived the terrible trauma you have vividly recalled.

The principle is: given that the experimenter is still alive to tell the tale, this fact is solid evidence that the 'stressed' has managed to survive even the most frustrating and threatening events that have actually happened to him.

This realistic fact should help the experimenter better tolerate present frustrations as the 'fantasized tragic hero' did not die but in fact lived to tell the tale.
It should be further supportive given the fact that if they could survive that witch they felt they could not might that not inspire them with hope and faith that they can with courage and determination they might be able to also tough out the present misfortune.

A major reason for man 'stressed' to being initially unmotivated is their negative attitude towards missed expectations (disappointments).

A negative attitude towards disappointments triggers off an automatic chain effect that starts with frustration and ends in despair. This automatic chain reaction that occurs in a split second is referred to as self esteem deregulation.

The antidote to self-esteem regulation is learning how to tolerate increasing dosages of frustration, anxiety, depression and stress.

Learning that you have a problem in self esteem regulation is a vital first step in changing by choosing to learn how to tolerate frustration, anxiety, depression, and stress. In so doing a person changes their negative attitudes to positive.

This next exercise enables a person how the experience of a disappointment turns into despair experienced as utter hopelessness.

Exercise – UM 2 - **Learning about Regulating & De-Regulating Your Self Esteem**

People who feel overwhelmed, discouraged, drained, helpless and hopeless experience their life's journey as aspiring so high and inevitably falling so low; or like the Myth of Sisyphus pushing a large rock up a mountain and once getting to the top the rock rolls back down to the bottom.

Another common narrative is: as one is walking along their life's road they unexpectedly fall into an open manhole, which was invisible. Once in the hole there is great sense of disorder, and confusion, Additional feelings are anxiety, depression, frustration and stress.

Being stuck once again is typically experienced with shock and alarm. There is a perceived gap between what one should reasonably expect (to have a reasonably smooth uninterrupted trip) versus what has actually happened (a surprise unwanted limiting diversion).

The PROCESS of SELF ESTEEM REGULATION (POSITIVE and NEGATIVE)

Self-esteem is not something a person has that is fixed for all time. Instead it is an active ongoing process which takes place day by day. An explanation of this process follows:

Everyone projects goals, ideals, wants as something to work towards attaining. These end points provide a sense of purpose, direction and focus by a person directing their energy through chosen action.

In between the attainment of a given goal is a gap beginning with the point of origin expressed as an idea, desire, wish, or want of something to be attained.

The gap between what is wanted versus what is currently available is either relatively small or relatively large.

A small gap between what is desired versus what is triggers off a series of feelings beginning with frustration.

A small gap triggers a relatively small amount of frustration. A big gap triggers a relatively intense intense feeling of frustration.

Frustration then triggers anger which in turn is turned in on the self.

Anger turned in on the self is experienced as depression.

very low energy. It is further accompanied by a belief that exercising almost any effort is futile.

The antidote to this automatic process of self-esteem deregulation is to slow down the whole process to slow motion. This enables the person who is affected by this to intervene at points along the process to ensure a positive and not negative result.

To this end, the first responder attempts to help the 'stressed' see how he actually creates low self-esteem by his negative attitudes to the various feelings he is experiencing.

The key insight is that disappointments of all kinds are inevitable facts of this life. No one is perfect and glitches occur to everyone all the time.

The key to success is being able to tolerate increasing dosages of frustration, anxiety, beginning with the point of origin expressed

as an idea, desire, wish, or want of something

to be attained.

The gap between what is wanted versus what is currently available is either relatively small or relatively large.

A small gap between what is desired versus what is triggers off a series of feelings beginning with frustration.

A small gap triggers a relatively small amount of frustration. A big gap triggers a relatively intense intense feeling of frustration.

Frustration then triggers anger which in turn is turned in on the self.

Anger turned in on the self is experienced as depression.

High self-esteem results when a person experiences their initial disappointments as a challenge to overcome their perceived obstacles.

Low self-esteem occurs when the reaction to disappointments is a sense of defeatism and negative inertia.

Low self-esteem is characterized by feelings of worthlessness, helplessness, hopelessness, depression, stress, disappointment, helplessness, hopelessness, and a number of other so called negative feelings.

One should not judge them as either pathological, or assertions of one's primary inadequacy or evidence of a severe character or personality disorder.

The task, of the first responder, if requested by the respondee is to trace his/her process of self- esteem deregulation.

This process always begins with identifying a disappointment (missed expectation) experienced as frustration.

Anger always follows frustration. The anger is then turned in on the self. The experience of anger turned in on the self is depression.

As the person is also disappointed that this process is happening beyond his control there is a parallel process which is frustrated by this realization leading to more anger turned into the self that is additionally frustrating.

The doubling of depression is experienced as despair resulting in predictable feelings of dejection, unworthiness, inadequacy, all earmarks of low self - esteem.

In this connection the first responder might ask:

(a) "Can you see how anger automatically follows when you get frustrated?"

(b) "Now where does your anger go meaning to where is it directed?"

(c) "Are you able to identify anger being turned in on yourself?"

(d) "Anger turned in on the self is experienced as depression. Can you feel it in yourself? "

(e) "How do you feel about the fact that this cycle happens all the time? What is your attitude towards it ?"

Once the cycle of self-esteem deregulation is identified and experienced by the respondee the first responder informs him that there is a pathway out of the bad feelings which requires his or her active participation in the five step discovery process.

The key to healthy self-esteem regulation is to be able to shift the persons' automatic attitude towards frustration from negative to accepting (positive).

The first responder then suggests appropriate exercises to accomplish this task.

Another approach to transforming the 'stressed' self-esteem deregulation process to a balanced self - esteem regulation process is to help them shift their attitude of hopelessness (experienced as quintessential stuckness) from negative to positive.

Attitude Shifting™

The First Responder directs the "stressed" to:

(a) Observe his attitude to not being able to overcome his sense of hopelessness, (or feeling overwhelmed, or sense of futility or whatever the missed expectation (disappointment happens to be).

   (b) A key issue resulting in a negative attitude to missed expectations (disappointments) is the perception that both inner and outer reality are only painted a depressing color of funereal deep purple.

   (c) It is as if the person with low self-esteem is viewing reality through glasses whose lenses are deep purple.

(d) People who are depressed characterized by feeling drained, hopeless, helpless need to at least intellectually that there are potentially better days ahead.

(e) In states of deep depression and despair it feels not only that this is the bed rock reality but that it may never change particularly if it has been going on sometimes for years.

These people need to feel that it is possible to get out of this resigned dark state. They need to believe that alternative exist that are better not just theoretically but potentially concrete for them.

The first responder explains that the person who feels hopeless and utterly overwhelmed who feels as if he is running on fumes is feeling depressed.

When one is depressed it is as if both internal and external reality are one unchanging funeral dark purple color. The antidote is for the dark purple lenses to be changed to clear.

EXERCISE –UM3 – How does Reality Really Look?

The first responder says the following:

(a) Imagine you are wearing a pair of eye glasses that have purple lens. Obviously all you would see would appear to be the same dark purple color.

(b) The first responder might go a step further by handing the 'stressed' two pairs of glasses. One pair has purple lenses; the other pair has plain glass lenses.

(c) How does reality look to you when you substitute the clear glass lens in place of the purple glass lens?

The point is to indicate to the 'stressed' that when depressed his/her sense of reality will be viewed through the influence of the dark color. Once the depression lifts dark color will turn to the normal variations.

Then the responder can inform the 'stressed' to hold onto the hope that there will be a brighter day once the depression lifts. If the 'stressed ' can accept this encouraging assertion they will be shift their attitude from being depressed about depression to accepting it automatically giving them a 'shot' of hope.

Attitude Shifting™

Conventional Approaches to Stress Management

Approaches Defined

Anxiety, depression and stress reduction is a hot topic.

Googling stress and anxiety produces thousands of references. Before introducing the reader to what's new in managing anxiety, depression, frustration and stress – it is valuable to survey the conventional approaches to this topic.

In this connection, managing stress, anxiety, frustration, and dreams depression has generated reams of self help guides along with offering numerous techniques such as meditation, Yoga, body work therapies etc. All of them work for some people.

The List

The following is a list of potential stress and anxiety reducers. Note that you have to experiment with what is most effective — if any — for you. They will differ with respect to how long lasting they are. Amplify — select and try. The list is in no particular order.

- Exercising
- "...No exercise..."
- Seriously, there are some places of great natural beauty around requiring just a tiny investment of driving time. Well worth it.
- So—here's the summary of your contributions, the compiled list:
- Stress Busters of the Therapists:
- Go to lunch with a friend
- Read for fun: light novels, mystery no vels, serious novels Exercise
- Don't exercise
- Walk your dogs
- Socialize with therapist friends
- Socialize with non-therapist friends
- Connect with family
- If you need to, cry
- Play cards
- Play dominos
- Go bowling

Attitude Shifting™

- Wear a great bowling shirt
- Practice T'ai Chi
- Watch others practice T'ai Chi
- Watch (good) bad movies and escapist TV shows on purpose
- Turn off the T.V. Spend relaxing time on the Computer.
- Turn off the computer
- Journal
- Get sufficient sleep
- Meditate
- Spend time in nature
- Tune into your faith, whatever that may be for you
- Rule out medical issues
- Clean something
- Paint a picture
- Paint your house
- Go rock climbing
- Get a massage
- Take a hot bath
- Smile at someone
- Practice random acts of kindness
- Pay for the food of the person in the drive-through behind you
- Honestly reassess your stress load, including your practice load
- Readjust your investment of/expenditure of

Attitude Shifting™

- Energy, if you need to
- Strive for balance
- Add some silly to your regimen
- Practice acceptance
- Veg out a little
- Cleanse your chakras
- Drink hot cocoa
- Take a news break
- Spend time alone
- Take a walk, by yourself or with a loved one
- or friend
- Find a soothing bedtime routine
- Make big pots of soup
- Chat with a friend on the phone
- Play a video game, online or by yourself
- Get a facial
- Get a Detox treatment
- Watch your favorite DVD
- Make a waiting list for your practice if you
- need to
- Hug a friend or loved one
- Engage in self-analysis to figure it out
- Go to therapy to figure it out
- Get supervision when necessary
- Indulge in a few extra carbs if you feel like it
- Get a good cup of coffee
- Consider a walking meditation
- Take nature photos

- Ride bikes
- Laugh
- Take in a comedy
- Treat yourself to a gelato
- Treat yourself to ice cream
- Listen to your favorite music
- Listen to silence
- Listen to nature
- Burn scented candles
- Put flowers round your room
- Go to the theatre, ballet or symphony
- Invest in some great jammies—silk, satin, or
- flannel, take your pick
- Open the curtains and let the sun stream in
- Bake bread
- View some beautiful visual art
- Get a bottle of your favorite wine or almond
- View some beautiful visual art
- Get a bottle of your favorite wine or almond
- champagne
- Go for the chocolate - 'nuff said
- When in doubt, ask a friend
- Practice gratitude
- Great list, everybody.
- [Get married] Those on the outside want to
- be inside
- [Get Divorced] Those on the inside want to
- be outside

Attitude Shifting™

- Take a hot bath
- Smile at someone
- Frown at someone
- Practice random acts of kindness
- Pay for the food of the person in the drive
- through behind you
- Honestly reassess your stress load, including
- your practice load
- Readjust your investment of/expenditure of energy if you need to
- Strive for balance
- Do something outrageous
- Add some silly to your regimen
- Practice acceptance
- Practice rejection

Whereas some of these exercises work well for many people for others they provide only limited relief.

You have to experiment with what is most effective for you. The exercises will differ with respect to how long their positive effects last. Select and try. If they work so be it. If they have been, or are, of limited benefit ....read on.

Some Limitations-Re Conventional Exercises

1. The major limitation of the list above is that their positive effects tend to be short lived. The reason for this is that the standard exercises reduce symptoms but fail to address causes. People suffering from the debilitating effects of stress and anxiety are best helped when the causes of their particular stress and anxiety are identified and mastered.

2. In many cases there are multiple causes that converge resulting in combinations of anxiety, depression, frustration and stress.

3. Many of the standard exercises require a great deal of attention and time to utilize them. Because most people in the grips of stress and anxiety are unable to focus as they literally are unable to think straight their

attention span is limited often interfering with completing the exercises.

4. Since there is a narrowing of focus for people who are stressed out and anxious they are often overwhelmed with too much information thrown at them. [Information overload].

Recognizing that many who are stressed out and anxious find the standard exercises listed above as too limiting, our Attitude Shifting™ picks up where conventional relaxation exercises leave off.

By contrast with conventional wisdom, our position is that the most effective stress and anxiety reducers are those that start with addressing primary causes rather than ending with reducing symptoms.

Common sense solutions might be to simply do nothing except wait for the ground to harden; put a wooden plank under the wheels; or call a tow truck.

Any of these rational solutions will work for these types of relatively uncomplicated problems. However, when it comes to solving the kind of complex problem faced by Joe in coping with the inevitable painful emotional states triggered by his multiple stressors, effective solutions often do not readily spring to mind.

Each of the suggested solutions for the car stuck in the mud problem presupposes a person being able to use his mind to come up with an effective problem solution.

This sounds good in theory, however many people in the grips of frustration, anxiety, and stress are unable to make use of this process as the chemicals in their mind (adrenalin) literally interfere with thinking clearly. In states of high stress and anxiety the mind literally cannot think straight and instead seems to be racing.

This is an important point as most advice about coping with these painful feelings assumes that people have the where with all to follow explicit directions in carrying out suggested exercises.

They often fail to mention that many people in the grips of anxiety, depression, intense frustration and stress are literally unable to focus their attention for more than a few minutes at a time.

Therefore – overwhelmed by a sense of urgency - they are likely to either give up or divert their attention in relatively short order as soon as they experience moving beyond their "fail safe" point.

A crucial implication follows: People trapped in a state of negative inertia need active intervention by a well meaning and hopefully well-informed 'helper' (first responder). Lending a helping hand to a person in need of help, most of the time, has the effect of stirring up potential kinetic energy in the inert person. Thus the reaching out of a caring helper often initiates a process whereby negative inertia is converted into positive momentum.

Attitude Shifting™ is designed to help professionals and any other helpers to effectively intervene in ways that will be maximally helpful to those in need of a helping hand. In so doing we believe that the key to success is in promoting the right attitude.

Recognizing that many who are stressed out and anxious find the standard exercises listed above as too limiting, our Attitude Shifting™ picks up where conventional relaxation exercises leave off.

By contrast with conventional wisdom, our position is that the most effective stress and anxiety reducers are those that start with addressing primary causes rather than ending with reducing symptoms.

If you desire long lasting relief identifying causes rather than settling for symptom relief Attitude Shifting™ should be your choice.

We Can Be Our
BROTHER'S KEEPER...

More Effectively by Utilizing the Information Contained in this Attitude Shifting™ Guide.

Attitude Shifting™

Additional Resources

Radio Programs

On Being

On Being is a spacious conversation — and an evolving media space — about the big questions at the center of human life, from the boldest new science of the human brain to the most ancient traditions of the human spirit. The program began as an occasional series on Minnesota Public Radio in 1999, then became a monthly national program in September 2001, and launched as a weekly program titled *Speaking of Faith* in the summer of 2003. [Issues of faith, hope, love, meaning, creativity, trust, spirituality, psychology.]
http://being.publicradio.org/ Krista Tippett: hostess

FORUMS

Health Forums - http://healthforums.org/

SUGGESTED BOOKS and ARTICLES

Relevant Books: web sites articles

Gibbsonline.com http://www.gibbsonline.com/

On Significant Psychological Change
http://www.gibbsonline.com/sigchange.html

Indicators of Significant Psychological Change
http://www.gibbsonline.com/indicies.html

Further Observations on Psychological Change -
http://www.gibbsonline.com/sigchange2.html

On Keeping a Personal Journal -
http://www.gibbsonline.com/journal.html

Coping With Fear - http://www.gibbsonline.com/coping.html

On Learning to Tolerate My Own Frustration -
http://www.gibbsonline.com/frustration.html

HONEST MEDICINE My Dream for the Future Dr. John Abramson's Overdosed America The Broken Promise of American Medicine (OR, How Medical Research Lost Its Credibility).mht

Campbell, Joseph · The Hero with a Thousand Faces
"The hero's act is to delve into the unconscious mind and bring it up and make it one with the conscious mind...[The modern hero is the person who explores the depths of his soul in psychoanalysis - accesses and faces his splits, and systematically works on himself to reconcile them.]

Durant, Will. The Story of Philosophy

Fromm, E. · Escape from Freedom
[Many humans conform because they are anxious when they feel free.]

Fraiberg, S. · The Magic Years
("Understanding and Handling the Problems of Early Childhood")

Frankel, Victor Logotherapy: From Death Camp to Existentialism

Daniel Goleman, *Emotional Intelligence* (1996) p. 43

Kaplan, L. · Oneness and Separateness: From Infant to Individual
[A detailed overview of the vicissitudes of identity formation in young children]

Karen Horney, The Neurotic Personality of Our Time (London 1977) p. 120

Karen Horney, New Ways in Psychoanalysis (London 1966) p. 254-5

Kierkegaard, S. · Fear and Trembling
"To venture causes anxiety, but not to venture is to lose one's self .... And to venture in the highest sense is precisely to become conscious of one's self."

May, Rollo · Man's Search for Himself
"Like the dinosaur, he had power without the ability to change, strength without the capacity to learn."

Spitz, R. · The First Year of Life
"Basic gratifications are closer to physiology than psychology. Security, provide for relief of need tension, relief from un-pleasure tension."

Williams, Gibbs. DEMYSTIFYING MEANINGFUL COINCIDENCES (SYNCHRONICITIES): The Evolving Self, The Personal Unconscious, and The Creative Process

Veterans Resources

VETERAN RESOURCES   http://www.ivaw.org/vetresources

MILITARY – VETERANS RESOURCES MANAGEMENT
http://www.vrna.org/

NAMI ALLIANCE ILLNESS PTSD MANAGEMENT
http://www.nami.org/Template.cfm?Section=Veterans_Resources&Template=/ContentManagement/ContentDisplay.cfm&ContentID=53242&lstid=877

NATIONAL SUICIDE PREVENTION LIFELINE – VETERANS RESORCE LOCATOR
http://www.suicidepreventionlifeline.org/Veterans/ResourceLocator.aspx

OTHER VETERANS RESOURCES ON THE WEB
http://www.archives.gov/veterans/other-resources/

THE NATIONAL RESOURCE DIRECTORY for WOUNDED, ILL, and INJURED SERVICE MEMBERS, VETERANS, and their FAMILIES
http://www.nationalresourcedirectory.gov/nrd/public/DisplayPage.do?parentFolderId=6006

US VETERANS RESOURCES   http://www.vetsresource.com/

VETS RESOURCE CONNECTION 2
http://nvti.cudenver.edu/VETSresource2/Default2.htm

ANXIETY RESOURCES

ANTI – ANXIETY SIDE EFFECTS

ANXIETY MEDICATIONS WHAT YOU NEED TO KNOW ABOUT ANTI-ANXIETY DRUGS
http://search.aol.com/aol/search?s_it=topsearchbox.afe&q=ANXIETY+MEDICATIONS

LIST OF ANTI-ANXIETY MEDICINES LIVESTRONG.COM
http://search.aol.com/aol/search?s_it=topsearchbox.afe&q=ANXIETY+MEDICATIONLIST%20;OF%20ANTI%20ANXIETY%20MEDICINES

PROS AND CONS OF ANTI-ANXIETY DRUGS
http://www.ehow.com/facts_4814118_pros-cons-antianxiety-medications.html

SIDE EFFECTS OF ANTI - ANXIETY DRUGS NEWSWEEK HEALTH
http://search.aol.com/aol/search?&query=side+effects+of+anti-anxiety&invocationType=tb50aoldesktopab

ANTI-ANXIETY DRUG TRENDS: CHILL PILLS -
http://search.aol.com/aol/search?&query=anti-anxioety+drug+trends&invocationType=tb50aoldesktopab

ANTI-ANXIETY MEDICATIONS CHART
http://www.healthyplace.com/anxiety-panic/treatment/anti-anxiety-medications-chart/menu-id-69/

ANXIETY and STRESS MANAGEMENT SITES

37 STRESS MANAGEMENT http://www.citehr.com/1918-37-stress-management-tips.html

ANXIETY MANAGEMENT http://www.anxietymanagement.com/

THE INTERNATIONAL ASSOCIATION FOR ANXIETY MANAGEMENT - http://www.anxman.org/

NATURAL ANXIETY MANAGEMENT http://www.way2hope.org/anxiety_management_help-natural.htm

NATIONAL PANIC and ANXIETY DISORDER NEWS http://www.npadnews.com/

ANXIETY and PANIC ATTACKS - http://www.anxietypanic.com/

MENTAL HEALTH LINKS: PSYCHOLOGY and PSCHIATRY - http://mentalhealth.samhsa.gov/links/default2.asp?ID=Psychiatry+and+Psychology&Topic=Psychiatry+and+Psychology

The Web's Stress Management & Emotional Wellness Page
file:///K:/Stress%20management%20on%20the%20web/Stress.htm

ALL DEPRESSION ARTICLES

http://www.everydayhealth.com/depression/all-articles.aspx?xid=GSLP&s_kwcid=TC|6122|anti%20depression%20side%20effects||S||3426799842&gclid=CPHzrKDsk54CFR9N5QodIWqAqA

MANAGING ANGER and FRUSTRATION

MANAGING ANGER AND FRUSTRATION
http://www.extension.org/pages/Managing_Anger_and_Frustration

POSITIVE PAYCHOLOGY: 5 TIPS MANAGING IMPATIENCE AND FRUSTRATION http://ke-mp.com/2007/10/03/positive-psychology-5-tips-on-managing-imaptience-and-frustration/

HOW to COPE WITH DEPRESSION AND FRUSTRATION for MANAGING STRESS - http://www.tipstrain.com/how-to-cope-with-depression-and-frustration-for-managing-stress/

NATIVE REMEDIES: THE NATURAL CHOICE – FRUSTRATION – http://www.nativeremedies.com/ailment/dealing-with-frustration-and-   discouragement.html

ADDICTION SITES

SUBSTANCE ABUSE and MENTAL HEALTH :

http://beta.helpguide.org/mental/health_substance_abuse_alcohol_depression_anxiety_addiction.htm

KICK OUT STRESS: http://kickoutstress.com/

STRESS MANAGEMENT:
http://www.einet.net/directory/4737/Stress_Management.htm

ANXIETY CENTER: http://www.anxietycentre.com/abuse-statistics-information.shtml

DRUG ADDICTION and STRESS: http://www.helpguide.org/mental/drug_substance_abuse_addiction_signs_effects_treatment.htm

STRESS HEALTH NETWORK: http://stresshealthnetwork.com/stressalcoholdruguse.html

DRUG ABUSE and ADDICTION: http://beta.helpguide.org/mental/drug_abuse_addiction_rehab_treatment.htm

POST TRAUMATIC STRESS DISORDER, RAPE, and SEXUAL ABUSE: http://www.buzzle.com/editorials/6-21-2006-100021.asp

DRUG ABUSE and DEPENDENCE: http://www.revolutionhealth.com/conditions/addiction/drug-abuse-recovery?section=section_04

MEDICINE NET. – STRESS : http://www.medicinenet.com/script/main/forum.asp?articlekey=488&articletype=hf

CREATIVE CARE'S BLOG: http://www.creativecareinc.com/blog/labels/Substance-Abuse.html

MANAGEMENT of SMOKING and STRESS and ANXIETY

ANXIETY, STRESS, and QUITTING SMOKING:
http://www.articlesbase.com/quit-smoking-articles/anxiety-stress-and-quitting-smoking-335279.html

E HEALTH FORUMS: PANIC and SOKING DISORDERS:
http://ehealthforum.com/health/smoking-and-panic-disorders-t150026.html

MANAGING EATING DISORDERS, STRESS and ANXIETY

COMPLICATIONS:
http://health.nytimes.com/health/guides/symptoms/stress-and-anxiety/complications.html

MANAGEMENT of JOB STRESS and ANXIETY

WEB MD- MANAGING JOB STRESS:
http://www.webmd.com/balance/stress-management/tc/managing-job-stress-topic-overview

STRESS at WORK:
http://helpguide.org/mental/work_stress_management.htm

STRESS and RELAXATION: http://www.stress-and-relaxation.com/

STRESS MANAGEMENT: http://www.squidoo.com/Stress-And-Management

Attitude Shifting™

MANAGING STRESS in the WORKPLACE:
http://www.infobarrel.com/Managing_Stress_Anxiety_in_the_Workplace

MANAGING DEBT, STRESS and ANXIETY

EIGHT TIPS FOR COPING WITH DEBT STRESS, ANXIETY, and DEPRESSION: http://www.uswitch.com/debt-help/coping-with-debt/

WEB MD- THE DEBT- STRESS CONNECTION: http://www.webmd.com/balance/features/the-debt-stress-connection

HOW to MANAGE YOUR STRESS in a BAD ECONOMY: http://www.healthyplace.com/anxiety-panic/articles/managing-your-stress-in-tough-economic-times/menu-id-69/

PLACEBOS and DRUGS

Placebos, Effects, What They are, How They Work
    Placebo Control Value to Medical Studies and Results Interpretation © Donald Reinhardt

WIRED MAGAZINE: 17.09

Placebos Are Getting More Effective. Drugmakers Are Desperate to Know Why. By Steve Silberman ▭08.24.09

http://www.wired.com/medtech/drugs/magazine/17-09/ff_placebo_effect?currentPage=all

Placebos Are Getting More Effective. Drugmakers Are Desperate to Know Why. By Steve Silberman ✉08.24.09

"Ironically, Big Pharma's attempt to dominate the central nervous system has ended up revealing how powerful the brain really is. The placebo response doesn't care if the catalyst for healing is a triumph of pharmacology, a compassionate therapist, or a syringe of salt water. All it requires is a reasonable expectation of getting better. That's potent medicine."

Contributing editor Steve Silberman (steve@stevesilberman.com) wrote about the hunt for Jim Gray in issue 15.08.
http://www.wired.com/medtech/drugs/magazine/17-09/ff_placebo_effect?currentPage=all

2 placebo effect

"The physician's belief in the treatment and the patient's faith in the physician exert a mutually reinforcing effect; the result is a powerful remedy that is almost guaranteed to produce an improvement and sometimes a cure." -- Petr Skrabanek and James McCormick, Follies and Fallacies in Medicine, p. 13.
http://www.skepdic.com/placebo.html

Enhancing the Placebo

By OLIVIA JUDSON   May 3, 2010, *10:07 pm*

Olivia Judson on the influence of science and biology on modern medicineplacebo effect

The placebo effect is, potentially, one of the most powerful forces in medicine. The challenge is to harness that power in a reliable and systematic way

…The problem is that humans are not machines, and emotions are not abstractions. Hope and expectation, anxiety and fear, trust and suspicion — these cause physiological changes in the brain that can interact with drugs, changing their effects.

http://opinionator.blogs.nytimes.com/2010/05/03/enhancing-the-placebo/

Notes:

The placebo effect has generated a vast and complex literature; my treatment of the topic is necessarily brief.

For anyone interested in a fascinating overview of the complexities of the placebo effect, see Moerman, D. 2002. "Meaning, Medicine, and the 'Placebo Effect.'" Cambridge University Press. I particularly recommend chapters 4 and 5; the first is on the importance of doctors, the second is on how different placebo regimes (pills, shots, surgery) compare with each other, and also how different regimens (taking pills four times a day as against once a day) can change the effectiveness of the placebo.

Anyone interested in the history of the placebo effect should read Shapiro, A. K. and Shapiro, E. 1997. "The Powerful Placebo: From Ancient Priest to Modern Physician." Johns Hopkins University Press. Note that the understanding of the physiology of the placebo effect has advanced considerably since this book was published.

A number of authors have written thoughtfully about enhancing the placebo effect. See, for example, Greene, C. S. et al. 2009. "Placebo responses and therapeutic responses. How are they related?" Journal of Orofacial Pain 23: 93-107; Finnis, D. G. et al. 2010. "Biological, clinical, and ethical advances of placebo effects." The Lancet 375: 686-695; and Miller, F. G., Colloca, L. and Kaptchuk, T. J. 2009. "The placebo effect: illness and interpersonal healing." Perspectives in Biology and Medicine 52: 518-539. See also Pacheco-López, G., et al. 2006. "Expectations and associations that heal: immunomodulatory placebo effects and its neurobiology." Brain, Behavior, and Immunity 20: 430-446.

For the 117 studies of ulcer drugs, see Moerman, D. E. 2000. "Cultural variations in the placebo effect: ulcers, anxiety, and blood pressure." Medical Anthropology Quarterly 14: 51-72. For physiological changes to the brain in response to the anticipation of receiving pain killers, see Colloca, L. and Benedetti, F. 2005. "Placebos and painkillers: is mind as real as matter?" Nature Reviews Neuroscience 6: 545-552; and Price, D. D., Finniss, D. G. and Benedetti, F. 2008. "A comprehensive review of the placebo effect: recent advances and current thought." Annual Reviews of Psychology 59: 565-590. This paper also discusses ways in which conditioning and memory may contribute to placebo responses. A number of papers have considered hidden versus open injections of drugs; for morphine in particular, see for example, figure 2 of Colloca, L. et al. 2004. "Open versus covert treatment for pain, anxiety, and Parkinson's disease." The Lancet Neurology 3: 679-684.

For expensive placebo pills being more effective than cheap ones, see Waber, R. L. et al. 2008. "Commercial features of placebo and therapeutic efficiency." Journal of the American Medical Association 299: 1016-1017. For sham devices being more powerful than placebo pills, see Kaptchuk, T. J. et al. 2006. "Sham device versus inert pill: randomised control trial of two placebo treatments." British Medical Journal 332: 391-394.

Sham surgery is controversial. For discussions of it, see Macklin, R. 1999. "The ethical problems with sham surgery in clinical research." New England Journal of Medicine 341: 992-996; and Johnson, A. G. 1994. "Surgery as a placebo." The Lancet 344: 1140-1142. For evidence of its power, see McRae, C. et al. 2004. "Effects of perceived treatment on quality of life and medical outcomes in a double-blind placebo surgery trial." Archives of General Psychiatry 61: 412-420; and Goetz, C. G. et al. 2008. "Placebo response in Parkinson's disease: comparisons among 11 trials covering medical and surgical interventions." Movement Disorders 23: 690-699.

Doctors' belief in the treatment can manifest itself in a variety of ways: if a doctor thinks the patient may have received a powerful painkiller, patients report less pain than if the doctor knows they have not. Similarly, a doctor's enthusiasm for a procedure often enhances its effect — for further information on this, see the Moerman book mentioned above. For the experiment involving the infusion of saline solution masquerading as a powerful drug, see Pollo, A.

et al. 2001. "Response expectancies in placebo analgesia and their clinical relevance." Pain 93: 77-84.

In general, prescribing placebo treatments is considered to be bad medicine (see a recent report by Britain's Parliament.*) For an alternative view, see Foddy, B. 2009. "A duty to deceive: placebos in clinical practice." American Journal of Bioethics 9: 4-12. For ways in which the placebo effect may be harnessed by "alternative" medical practices, see Kaptchuk, T. J. 2002. "The placebo effect in alternative medicine: can the performance of a healing ritual have clinical significance." Annals of Internal Medicine 136: 817-825.*

Many thanks to everyone who has listened to my musings on the placebo effect, and to Mike Eisen for pointing out the study of Brazilians versus Germans. But particular thanks are due to Sofia Castello y Tickell, Dan Haydon, and Jonathan Swire for insights, **comments and suggestions.**

Made in the USA
Charleston, SC
26 October 2013